# Praise for *Defining Moments: Insights into the Lawyer's Soul*

"Inspirational! At every turn, Melanie Bragg meaningfully touches the reader. Lawyers and non-lawyers who read this book will be changed for the better."
—Randall O. Sorrels, Partner, Abraham, Watkins, Nichols, Sorrels, Agosto & Aziz, President, State Bar of Texas, 2019–2020

"Melanie Bragg's *Defining Moments: Insights into the Lawyer's Soul* is an incredible collection of stories by lawyers about lawyers. The stories strip away the law, the education, the role of the attorney and rather uncover the real person underneath the lawyer. The reader gets the insight of what motivated or compelled each individual to study and practice law. The stories display the historical angst around gender, race, and age from a very personal level. I was swept up in each one, wanting them to last longer and then refreshingly engaged with a brand new one. I'll be a customer and keep it on my bookshelf for years to come."
—Elizabeth Pudwill, Assistant to the Editor, Houston Chronicle

"With her book *Defining Moments: Insights into the Lawyer's Soul*, Melanie Bragg masterfully proves that attorneys do their work in a heartfelt and empathetic way. Bragg gives us living proof that the law and love go hand in hand to serve our people."
—John Koehler, publisher at Koehler Books, author of seven books

"Prepare to take a journey of self-awareness and enlightenment. Melanie shows us how to embrace adversity and to use it as a springboard for personal growth and resilience. How we rebound through seemingly impossible waves will define us and help propel us forward. *Defining Moments* presents a deeply personal and candid anthology of lessons learned over several lifetimes. It instructs us on how to find our own points on the horizon to guide us through anything life throws our way. Each inspirational chapter teaches us how to look beyond our near-term challenges, to embrace the experience and grace of others, and see the uplifting and lasting effect of caring for and helping others—which is, after all, the touchstone of our great profession."
—Arvin Maskin, Attorney, Weil, Gotshal & Manges, LLP, New York, New York

"*Defining Moments* is a magnificent book that shares inspiring stories from numerous legal luminaries. Melanie Bragg's love of the law shines through on every page and her wisdom serves as a beacon of bright light for lawyers and nonlawyers alike. This is a must-read for everyone in search of practical insights on how to put passion, possibility, and purpose to work."
—Kathleen Welton, Producer, aka Associates, Chicago, Illinois

"Melanie Bragg serves up a big bowl of nourishing chicken soup for the soul of all lawyers, from those starting out to those nearing retirement. In *Defining Moments: Insights into the Lawyer's Soul*, lawyers of all stripes share personal experiences and life tips in short essays that will delight and nurture everyone, all wrapped up delightfully with Melanie's own brand of optimism and can-do spirit. A must!"
—Robert C. Paul, Attorney, East Hampton, NY

"Melanie Bragg's *Defining Moments: Insight's into the Lawyer's Soul* is a chorus of unique voices singing in harmony with inspirational, uplifting, and empowering stories reminding us that the practice of law is truly a service profession. In keeping with this truth, Bragg serves her fellow lawyers by presenting their wisdom and insights in a two- to three-page format that is perfect for use in a five-minute daily mindfulness routine."
—Kellye C. More, Partner, Walker Hulbert Gray & Moore, LLP, Perry, Georgia

"In *Defining Moments*, Melanie Bragg explores the human side of the lawyer's psyche. As she breaks through the stereotypes associated with attorneys and their attitudes toward the world, she exposes the experiences that shaped each of those interviewed. The stories reveal moments in each lawyer's past that led them to what Bragg calls LEAD: Legacy, Excellence, Authenticity, and Determination. This book should be added to every law library in the country so that new barristers can aspire to the greatness of each of these attorneys and realize the sense of balance that is possible in their budding careers. It can also serve any author aspiring to write legal fiction as a deep dive into understanding what motivates attorney's and how they think."
—Manning Wolfe, Attorney and Author of the Merit Bridges Legal
  Thriller Series

"An inspiring and entertaining read. Attorney and author Melanie Bragg interviewed many of the country's leading lawyers and has masterfully woven their diverse tales of how and why they chose the legal profession around the central theme of how leaders are made. She has found that the common traits of these lawyers can be found in the acronym LEAD: Legacy, Excellence, Authenticity, and Determination. Do yourself a favor and read *Defining Moments* today!"
—Lynn Allingham, Attorney, Anchorage, Alaska

"*Defining Moments* captures hundreds of inspirational thoughts and ideas that lift and encourage us at a time when the reputation of our profession is tarnished by the disheartening choices of a few. . . . Truly a gem, these stories will remain with you long after you've read them. Some bring smiles, some tears. They all help us remember why we work so hard to ensure that equal justice for all is not a concept but reality."
—L. Terry, Attorney Oklahoma City, Oklahoma

"*Defining Moments, Insights into the Lawyer's Soul*, is a literary masterpiece 'for such a time as this.' Sharing stories that change lives and reshape the narrative of a profession is no easy task. It takes courage and skill to identify pertinent life chronicles that humanize and lend a transparent dignity to the legal profession. Melanie Bragg is a master storyteller and evidence of her ability to recognize a good story that will leave a literary legacy for young lawyers in the decades to come is exhilarating."
—Sharon C. Jenkins, Inspirational Principal, The Master Communicator's Writing
  Services, Houston, Texas

"*Defining Moments* is an inspiration. It will not only help young lawyers identify their passion but will uplift and encourage every reader to live from their heart. Bragg's wisdom and compassion shines through in each interview."
—Susan Jeffrey Busen, bestselling author of *Bridging Medicine and Miracles*
  and *Tormented by Technology*, Chicago, Illinois

*"Defining Moments* showcases the inspirations, challenges, and pivotal life experiences that have made lawyers true leaders in the profession. Melanie Bragg expertly weaves these stories into a rich and powerful tapestry of lawyers who bring purpose and a sense of mission to their day-to-day lives. Melanie has written an exceptional book about exceptional people!"
—**Richard "Rick" Paszkiet, Content Guy, Business Law Section,**
**American Bar Association, Chicago, Illinois**

"Melanie Bragg has envisioned and compiled a great reference tool for lawyers to learn about who they are and how they can be of service to the world better, as lawyers and people. *Defining Moments* shows that as lawyers, we must remember we are humans and that we matter as such."
—**Katy Goshtasbi, JD, CEO Puris Consulting, San Diego, California**

*"Defining Moments: Insights into the Lawyer's Soul* is like a *Profiles in Courage* for lawyers and anyone interested in the law. It provided true insights into the lives and souls of the lawyers I know. For those I don't, I definitely want to meet them. Melanie Bragg's interviews and narratives are fantastic. I have written down many of the LEAD lines to inspire me in the future."
—**Karen Goodman, Attorney and Past President, California Women Lawyers**

"This extremely practical and useful book reveals how some of America's most outstanding lawyers used personal experiences to improve their lives and overcome challenges. Melanie Bragg has put together a fantastic book with a wealth of information that will inspire, motivate, and encourage you to be the best lawyer you can be."
—**David H. Lefton, Esq., Lawyer Barron Peck Bennie & Schlemmer,**
**Chair GP Solo 2017, Cincinnati, Ohio**

"Melanie Bragg has tapped the minds of brilliant lawyers who share meaningful experiences and motivations in their practices and their lives. When you read their stories, you will feel proud to be part of the such a selfless profession. You will be re-energized about why you chose the law and will reflect on the moments and people who have shaped your path to becoming a lawyer."
—**Lynne A. Ustach, Esq., New Britain, Connecticut**

"In *Defining Moments*, Melanie Bragg propels her audience into a personal defining moment. One in which the experiences of her interviewees lead to many 'Aha!' moments as only wonderful epiphanies may excite. The journey through *Defining Moments*, through Legacy, Excellence, Authenticity, and Determination causes both laughter and tears as the realization that those experiences are as human and emphatic as one's own. An excellent source for inspiration and reflection!"
—**Robin Scott, Attorney at Law, Houston, Texas**

"After 40 years, I still wrestle with the question, What was that defining moment? When all the long days and sleepless nights, the unrealistic expectations of clients, the family sacrifices, and the uncompromising adversarial opponent were worth it. In *Defining Moments*, it all made sense. A career in law is not one moment but a lifetime of events, experiences, challenges, and most important self-reward. Whether you are beginning your career or beginning to reflect, Melanie Bragg's collection of essays resonates with the message that it was well worth it."
—**Benjamin H. Berkley, Attorney and Author of the legal thriller, *In Defense of Guilt***

"*Defining Moments* by Melanie Bragg is a commanding book. It is an easy read. The personal stories are impressive, yet thought-provoking. At the conclusion, you sit back and think, 'WOW, how can I implement into my life the lessons explored and examined by the authors?' *Defining Moments* gives one the insight into how to develop their own LEAD line."
—Rita K. Borzillo, Esquire, Faculty & MBA Director, Eastern University, St. David's PA

"Lawyers are often much-maligned and often viewed as the least-trusted professionals, but in Melanie Bragg's latest book, *Defining Moments*, we see this stereotype upended when we read real-life cases of attorneys with true heart and soul, forging strength from personal trauma and using the resulting growth to fuel their desire to affect others and make a real difference in the world. This should be required reading for all law students!"
—Geoff Akins-Hannah, Inspirational Entertainer of *The Bubble Wonders Show*

"Melanie Bragg hits the nail on the head with 42 compelling interviews revealing the attributes of leaving a legacy for those who follow you, the importance of excellence and authenticity in our dealings with others, and the value of determination to reach one's goals. This is an excellent template for all lawyers to follow."
—Tom Sweeney, Attorney, Clark Hill PLC, Birmingham, Michigan

"Melanie Bragg has authored an insightful book with a perspective of attorneys seldom seen. I was moved by this book. Many of the stories reveal lawyers to be emotionally intelligent people who understand the importance of how they treat others and the imperative to be fair and just from the heart. This book is valuable to lawyers and nonlawyers alike and will move readers to re-examine their own values and response to *Defining Moments*!"
—Eddie Turner, The Leadership Excelerator® (Executive Coach and Keynote Speaker)

"*Defining Moments: Insights into the Lawyer's Soul* provides wonderful insight from a diverse group of interesting lawyers. There are entertaining 'war stories' and great words of wisdom. These lawyers from all backgrounds, with varying reasons for entering the law profession, have all enjoyed success. It is interesting to read how each recognize and define those successes. *Defining Moments* is a great read for anyone and the perfect gift for the lawyer or law student in your life."
—Warren W. Harris, Partner, Bracewell LLP, President, Houston Bar Association

"*Defining Moments* is a revealing look at the working lawyer and the issues they face. I love how my friend Melanie Bragg has put together this fresh look at the profession and people who labor in it every day for others."
—W. Terry Whalin, bestselling author of more than 60 books

"*Defining Moments* is a must read book for everyone, not just lawyers. The stories told in this book are so insightful, heartfelt, and meaningful. The accomplishments that are written about in *Defining Moments* are amazing. Melanie has hit a homerun with this incredibly inspirational book."
—Kari M. Petrasek, Owner, Petrasek Law, PLLC, Mukilteo, Washington

# MELANIE BRAGG

# DEFINING MOMENTS

## INSIGHTS INTO THE LAWYER'S SOUL

ANKERWYCKE

The materials contained herein represent the opinions of the authors and/or the editors, and should not be construed to be the views or opinions of the law firms or companies with whom such persons are in partnership with, associated with, or employed by, nor of the American Bar Association unless adopted pursuant to the bylaws of the Association.

Nothing contained in this book is to be considered as the rendering of legal advice for specific cases, and readers are responsible for obtaining such advice from their own legal counsel. This book is intended for educational and informational purposes only.

Printed in the United States of America.

23 22 21 20 19 5 4 3 2 1

Library of Congress Cataloging-in-Publication Data

Names: Bragg, Melanie, author.
Title: Defining Moments : Insights into the Lawyer's Soul / written and edited by Melanie Bragg.
Description: Chicago : American Bar Association, 2019. | Includes index.
Identifiers: LCCN 2019006074 (print) | LCCN 2019006484 (ebook) | ISBN 9781641054201 (epub) | ISBN 9781641051095 (hardcover)
Subjects: LCSH: Lawyers—United States—Biography. | Practice of law—United States. | Law—Vocational guidance—United States.
Classification: LCC KF353 (ebook) | LCC KF353.B695 2019 (print) | DDC 340.092/273—dc23
LC record available at https://lccn.loc.gov/2019006074

Discounts are available for books ordered in bulk. Special consideration is given to state bars, CLE programs, and other bar-related organizations. Inquire at Book Publishing, ABA Publishing, American Bar Association, 321 N. Clark Street, Chicago, Illinois 60654-7598.

www.shopABA.org

*This book is dedicated to my father, Charles V. Bragg, who told me, "Get your law degree and then you can do whatever you want to do after that." I am forever grateful to him for his insight because I found the best career in the law and have experienced things I could never have envisioned as a young girl. Having that parent who believes in you and cheers you on is invaluable. Thank you, Daddy!*

# Contents

# PART 2
# Excellence

# PART 3
## Authenticity

# PART 4
## Determination

# Foreword

In *Defining Moments: Insights into the Lawyer's Soul* Melanie has captured the essence of some of the most outstanding lawyers in the legal community to illustrate the dynamic reality of the practice of law and the incredible demands it places on the human spirit and the physical body. No effort of this magnitude goes without a cost and lawyers know the high price of success. There is little margin for error when prosecuting a legal case or defending an innocent victim. Lawyers have the ability to fashion the law and thus affect every area of life—from our infrastructure, to our legal systems, to our legislative work, our education, our health, and more. The boundaries of the law are infinite, and the lawyers Melanie highlights in this book are examples of the best of the legal practice in America, covering a variety of areas of practice, geography, and time periods.

The "LEAD Line" is a success principle for lawyers and really any profession to follow in their practices and their daily life. Just by incorporating these LEAD lines into your daily life you will see a shift in your energy, and you will begin to experience better outcomes.

Having written and edited more than 200 *Chicken Soup for the Soul®* books, I know very well the time and effort it takes to interview people and to distill their words into meaningful stories. The depth and breadth of these lawyers' lives and their vulnerabilities are presented in such a way that nearly every reader can relate. When Melanie began this project, she wisely asked me how to get the people she was going to interview to be vulnerable and transparent in their interviews. I told her that the secret to getting people to be vulnerable, was to be open and vulnerable herself. From the quality of the stories in this book, I can see that she took my advice.

Before Melanie became Chair of the Solo, Small Firm and General Practice Division of the American Bar Association, she brought her leadership team to my hometown of Santa Barbara to spend a few days of meeting and planning. I had the pleasure of working with the group for one of those days and teaching them some of the principles of success I have learned. Later the next year I got to know the group more deeply when I was asked to be a keynote speaker at the Joint Young Lawyers Division/GPSolo Fall Conference in Charleston, South Carolina. I spent three days and nights with both young and older lawyers from all over the United States. During that time, I learned a lot about lawyers and the service they provide in their communities. As a result, I now have a greater appreciation for the work they do and the stresses the profession places on them. When you finish reading this book, you will too.

I believe *Defining Moments: Insights into the Lawyer's Soul* should be a must read for all lawyers and the public they serve. Lawyers have complex, deep, and insightful lives that we can all learn from and grow as we work on making the world a better place.

Jack Canfield
Coauthor of the *Chicken Soup for the Soul®* series
and *The Success Principles™: How to Get from Where You Are to Where You Want to Be*

# Acknowledgments

There are so many people to thank for their support in editing and writing this book. Let me see if I can do justice to some of them.

To Jack Canfield for being such a supportive and knowledgeable mentor. I envisioned this book and he agreed to help me figure out how to do it. Who better to mentor you than someone who has written and edited all of the *Chicken Soup for the Soul®* books? I thank Jack for teaching me how to get over my fears and tackle big projects. The interviewing process is an art form that you develop over time and like anything else it takes practice. Jack Canfield has given me endless support and mentorship and I thank him.

I owe a lifelong debt of gratitude to every one of the amazing interviewees in this book. Many of the people I interviewed are old friends of mine, people I have admired and grown up with for the past thirty years of my involvement in the American Bar Association. I am touched by the amount of vulnerability they showed by opening up their hearts and lives to me. They participated in the project even though they did not know when it was going to happen or how I was going to do it. There were numerous interviews where we both cried, it was so emotional.

Thank you to each and every one of the lawyers who are in this book. You are a credit to our profession and to humanity in general.

Thank you to the American Bar Association Publishing for publishing this book. ABA Publishing is the gold standard for legal publishing. And the ABA is the international standard for the practice of law and is the leader in setting an example of the rule of law in the world. The structure and organization of the organization is vast, and it has served many in so many ways. We must realize that without our national ABA structure and voice, the profession would not be where it is today.

I have had the support of the ABA for this project and having served on the Book Publications Board of the Solo, Small Firm and General Practice Division since 2005 and chairing it from 2012 to 2015, I had the honor of working side by side with the next person to whom I owe much gratitude and acknowledgment, Richard "Rick" Paszkiet, Content Guy, Business Law Section.

Rick led our GPSolo book board for many years, and during that time we shared a deep love of books and of nurturing authors from submission to publication. When I first started doing the interviews Rick said to me, "You are going to be the Studs Terkel of the law." I responded, "Who is Studs Terkel?" I spent a couple of hours on the Chicago Historical Society website and realized what an incredible compliment that was. I became a fan of Studs Terkel. I watched the interviews he conducted at age ninety-six and was astounded that we shared so many opinions. He discussed how nervous people are when they are talking about themselves and how being human and showing your vulnerability was the way to make them feel comfortable. In his interview, Richard "Racehorse" Haynes echoed this same technique in his trial strategy. What started out as a mistake—when he accidentally "kicked the spittoon" and the jury laughed—became something he did in every trial to break the ice with jurors.

Another person I must thank from the bottom of my heart is my good friend and collaborator of all things publishing, Bryan L. Kay, ABA Publishing Director, Editorial and Licensing. Bryan has been an endless source of support for this project. He never rushed me or pushed me to get it done when I felt like a part of my heart was being cut out by leaving anything out of an interview. His confidence in me trumped my insecurities over and over and I thank him for that.

Another close friend and confidante I want to thank is Kathleen Welton, publishing executive. I have looked up to Kathleen since I walked the aisles at the Book Expo with her in 2005. Everyone knew Kathleen and she was the fastest walker I had ever met, besides me. We stood in line to wait to talk to Jack Canfield and were so excited about this project. Her confidence in me has helped immensely.

I thank my new editor John Palmer, ABA Executive Editor, Flagship Division, for pushing all the buttons to get this book out timely for me as I juggle my law practice and chairing the GPSolo Division. He has been supportive and great to work with. I also want to thank my staff at GPSolo for their endless support of my publications and love of books—Kim Kocian, Executive Director; Steve Wildi; and Sherri Napue.

The real work of this book has been going on a long time. Getting the long interviews transcribed and edited was not easy. I acknowledge and praise my good friend and longtime legal secretary, Ivy Rosenberg, for her help. Ivy has tirelessly transcribed and edited the interviews, helped me with Excel spreadsheets and has given me critical advice on what she likes and doesn't like about the interviews during this whole process. I share our story in keynotes now when explaining how Jack Canfield's Success Principle #17, ASK, ASK, ASK, works. I'll explain.

When I first began the project, I needed the interviews transcribed. Ivy told me she could not do it. I came back a month later and asked a different way and the answer was still no. That went on for eight months. I asked every way I could. I bribed. I begged. But I never gave up and when she finally said yes, the rest is history. She tells me to tell my audiences when I talk about rejection and how to handle it, that it wasn't that she didn't want to help me, it was just that it wasn't a good time for her. I am glad I had the tenacity to stick with it because I could not have done this book and project without her. She laughed and cried along with me and was an endless source of support. Thank you, Ivy, for sticking with me.

There are so many other people to thank who support me in my efforts to write and speak more: My law clerks along the way who have helped edit the interviews and have done everything else while I worked on the book, Ashley Hallene, Mackenzie Coplen, and Laura Beth Brown. Laura Beth helped with the organization and worked closely with Ivy to get the project in order before we did the final edit. Sarah Lonvick, helped me bring this book home. I love everything in the interviews, so it was tough for me to cut. Sarah is a talented writer and will go far in her legal career.

And last, I want to thank my family and friends for the support they have given me in my quest to learn and grow as a lawyer and as a person and to share what I have learned with a wider audience. So often, I could not go to an event or come home for the holidays because I was working on this project and I thank you for understanding about my passion and drive to communicate. I hope the results here demonstrate it was worth it!

# Introduction

Defining moments in our lives are those touchpoint moments when something inside us shifts and we know that our world is profoundly different than it was before. The incidents are often small, and it is often not until later in life when you are asked to reflect, that you realize how important a person or an event was to your overall focus in life. These defining moments are like the clothespins that hold up the tapestry of our lives.

In 2003 I took my first Best-Selling Authors program from Jack Canfield in Santa Barbara. He was busy writing *Success Principles* then. In class, I asked him why he never did a "Chicken Soup for the Lawyer's Soul" book. With his affable, quick wit he quipped, "You know, wouldn't a 'Chicken Soup for the Lawyer's Soul' book kind of be like the book *What Men Know About Women*, you know the one where you open the pages and there is nothing on them?" Everyone in our class laughed and although I knew he was joking I think the seed for this book came from that defining moment. I knew lawyers did have souls and I wanted to write about them and study them as a way of leading and encouraging others to improve their lives and practices.

Getting lawyers to open up and talk about what is real and meaningful is not easy. We are taught to be strong and fierce and letting our guard down is not something that we do very often. I asked Jack how to get people to be vulnerable in the interviews and he said, "If you want them to be vulnerable, you need to be vulnerable." That comment stuck with me and in our interviews, I revealed much of myself too.

I began to interview friends of mine in the legal community about their defining moments. My curiosity drove me to wonder whether there was a pattern in successful people's lives and if there was a leadership model I could share with others to help them achieve their goals and dreams. Learning what experiences shaped them and identifying patterns in their stories would surely help motivate, encourage, and inspire other professionals. There is no way that I can cover the depth and breadth of these lawyers' lives in this short book. The point is to give you the stories around the LEAD line that shaped them.

Hearing about them and seeing how their LEAD lines operated in their lives has been an inspirational experience for me. Sharing it with you is an awesome joy and privilege. My goal is for you to identify your LEAD lines and begin living from your highest self in order to achieve your life's purpose. You may want to adopt some of them too.

When I began to think about LEAD lines, I broke the word "lead" down into four main leadership principles: Legacy, Excellence, Authenticity, and Determination.

Once I had the four leadership principles, a pattern developed. The stories naturally gravitated into these four categories. I am grateful for the many amazing lawyers who are included in the book. Their back stories—the experiences that formed the basis of their lives—point us to events that triggered their most profound, life-changing moments where a pivot was required to broaden their horizons and get them to where they are today.

The key component that distinguishes leaders is how they overcome and use their life struggles to grow and advance themselves, their families, and their communities. Everyone has difficulties as you will see in these stories. We often look at highly successful people and think it was all champagne and roses along the way. Many of the lawyers in this book have overcome insurmountable odds.

Anyone who thinks that lawyers are not the greatest group of public servants and philanthropists will have to think twice after reading this book. People who told me they had nothing to say were often astounded at what they shared. My interviews only confirmed what I knew: Lawyers are not only natural leaders, but they are also givers and hard workers. You see them serving in philanthropic positions in their profession and communities all across the country every day and yet the public is often unaware of the good they do. Leadership is engrained in the legal profession, and every lawyer is in some way, each day, being a leader.

My research reveals they all got there the same way everyone else did, with their own childhood issues, rejections, disappointments and tragedies, but they overcame them and rose up to achieve their goals. Everyone is a work in progress, and I am honored to be able to show you glimpses into the lives of some of the top lawyers in America today, and some that are no longer with us, who leave a legacy for us to learn valuable life lessons.

Since the day I graduated law school I knew I was entering the world's greatest profession and from now, many years later, I still feel the same way. This book has given me the opportunity to get to know many great lawyers and explore their backgrounds in more depth, and the more I learned about the lawyers, many of whom are my friends, the more respect and admiration I had for the profession as a whole and what motivates us as members of a great society that strives to help make the world go around in new and better ways.

I have been lucky enough to be involved in the American Bar Association since 1986 when, as a young lawyer and representative of the Houston Young Lawyers Association (I had the honor of serving as the first female President in 1990–91), I attended the infamous Montreal Young Lawyers Division (YLD) meeting. I was impressed and awed by what was going on there. Shortly thereafter, I was appointed Vice-Chair of the Juvenile Justice committee under the chair, William P. Hogan, by the then YLD Chair, William P. Hubbard, who became an ABA President many years later. I eventually became a Director of the Young Lawyers Division under then Chair, Judy Perry Martinez, who is one of our interviewees and will be the ABA President in 2019–20.

In my many years in the legal profession, I began to see a pattern of success and realized that everyone has an individual way of doing things. There are many paths to success. I wanted to talk to lawyers from all walks of life and in different practice settings and really find out what makes them tick. The interviews are a treasure trove of interesting autobiographical information about some of the brightest legal minds and successful lawyers in America. I had a goldmine of leadership information to pass on not only to lawyers but also to women and men in all professions. This harmonious blend of stories is a leadership manual for any entrepreneur or person who wants to learn the secrets of getting ahead and enjoying life to its fullest.

I hope you enjoy these stories and can see yourself in the history, the experiences, and the trials and tribulations of the great lawyers herein. My goal is to inspire you, to motivate you, and to encourage you to be the best person you can be and to find joy and meaning in your life each day.

The acronym for the LEAD line leadership model is: Legacy, Excellence, Authenticity, Determination.

## Legacy

Legacy is the first prong of the LEAD line model of leadership. We often think of legacy in terms of heirs to our property or how much of an estate we leave to our children or what extraordinary, heroic things we do that merit special recognition. Programs we start that remain after we are gone; children we birth; books we write. As I see and experience more and more of life, I realize that legacy is a living, breathing NOW thing. It occurs in the moment and can be measured in both big and small ways. Each kind act, whether it be a smile to a suffering stranger, or a favor done when no one is looking contributes to your legacy and builds the foundation for a profound spiritual legacy that cannot be measured in dollars and cents.

Lawyers are lucky because the opportunities to produce and influence legacy abound in untold ways every day. As Alan Kopit says in his interview, your legacy is the number of lives you change.

You just have to be aware of them, recognize them, and appreciate them for what they are. Look around at your life and think of all the ways you have been able to create legacy. Whether it be in the training of competent staff, nurturing law students and young associates to achieve their highest dreams, or by helping a client get a good result. If you begin to consider this, you will find many ways that you are creating your own legacy each and every day.

## Excellence

Excellence is the second prong of the leadership model. The law is an area where excellence is required. Having been through the rigorous training in law for three years after college, the practice of attending to details and making sure you get it right is ingrained in most lawyers' heads. As our interviews reveal, the path to becoming excellent can be filled with potholes and as Mr. Perdue says, "Out of the hottest furnace comes the hardest steel." Excellence contains many life lessons and it is something that we can keep refining each day as we follow the LEAD lines we learn in the interviews.

## Authenticity

As the interviews will reveal, we often wait for others to tell us what they will us to do and we may do things for the wrong reasons because we are not being authentic. The road to becoming authentic is not a straight line. But if you continue down the path, you will get there and be so much happier. As Barbara Mayden says in her interview, "Find your voice because no one is going to give it to you." As lawyers, we have many opportunities to blend in, but we also have opportunities to make waves. The concepts explored in the interviews form a picture of how others found their way to authenticity and I hope it will give you many ideas of how to find it for yourself too. The inner peace you have from living your own truth and for being who you know you were born to be will be your reward.

## Determination

No great thing was ever accomplished without much effort. And with effort there needs to be flexibility, the ability to come up against all odds and overcome them. The interviewees in these stories faced tough situations of all sorts and how they handled them and their results will be an inspiration to all. There is a saying that the darkest hour is before the dawn. So many give up on their dreams before they fulfill them, or they just get lost in the mundane day-to-day of life and it passes without their actually reaching their goals and dreams. My story is in this area of determination because I feel that is the one quality that, without it, you can't succeed. Nothing worth having is easy, as we know from studying for the bar exam. Flunking the bar, being an immigrant child who could not speak English, being someone who was discriminated against because of the color of their skin all give rise to a choice: Are you going to quit or are you going to stay in the game? Great lawyers are made from those who persevere and stand up for themselves and what they believe in.

There is a wide range of experience among the lawyers' stories herein. I have not told you all of their accomplishments, those can easily be found online. I wanted to stick with the nuts and bolts of what shaped them and what brought them to the point today where they are fighting for what is right in our society and giving it their all. They are all heroes.

# PART 1
# Legacy

# One Hand Extended Can Make a Difference

*Judy Perry Martinez*

Judy grew up in a middle-class family in New Orleans, Louisiana. Her father owned a furniture store in the Upper Ninth Ward. She went through the Catholic school system from elementary through high school. "I grew up with the influence of parents who were very, very involved with their children and their lives and who supported them through everything—from sports and dance for me, and sports and Cub Scouts for the boys, and everything in between." She had a grandmother living in the house too, who she credits for much of her upbringing.

Later in life, after Judy's father died, her mother moved in with Judy, Judy's husband, Rene, and their four children. "I think having that elder parent in your home gives you an opportunity to send messages to your children through your own acts and that of the grandparent about love, respect, politeness, and genuine kindness. A grandparent is a person who also can share in the duties and responsibilities of raising a child. I refer back to the often-quoted Hillary Clinton phrase that 'it takes a village to raise a child.' That was very much what it was like in my home where I grew up as well as in my home where my husband, Rene, and I raised our four children with the benefit of my mother living with us. Plus, I had a very close and engaged mother-in-law who ended up being my mother's best friend in life for many years."

I asked her about her public service roots because I first met Judy when I was the law student director of the Texas Young Lawyers Association and she came to one of our meetings on behalf of the ABA Young Lawyers Division. In August 2019, she will begin her year as president of the ABA. She told me, "As for public service, that started very, very early on. My parents were always very supportive of their community in St. Bernard parish and very involved in their church. My father was somebody who, while not on the political side, but just on the helping side, was always giving out a hand. Because of their attitudes of always helping others, we all were interested in helping when we saw a need. We had a young neighbor, Stevie, who had Down syndrome. He was loved by everyone in the neighborhood. We had twenty-six children in a square block of our neighborhood—five girls and twenty-one boys. We were always together. Our parents were always together, and Stevie was a big part of it. My brother, Al, who is a lawyer who practices in Louisiana, served as the first president of a Louisiana state youth chapter of a national organization serving children with intellectual disabilities, now known as the ARC. With the help of special education teachers in the area while he was in his first years of high school, he started an annual summer camp for children who had Down syndrome and autism. I really admired my brother for doing so much then.

She continues, "Most of the kids in the neighborhood worked as camp counselors and Al got more kids involved. Our summer activity was to staff his camp. The camp served kids with intellectual challenges and autism, some of them severely so, but we brought them every day to camp on a bus. We brought them to putt-putt, swimming, movies, and skating. Al realized in later years that the young people who went to the camp never attended a senior prom. So with lots of help and guidance from special education teachers and parents, he started a senior prom for the teenagers who were mentally challenged in New Orleans. It was held at a big hotel in downtown New Orleans with food and a band. The attendees all received corsages and boutonnières and wore formals and tuxedoes. Because of that experience and leadership, Al went on to start the state chapter of the ARC. Several years later, I followed in his footsteps and became head of the camp and head of the state chapter when I was a freshman at LSU in Baton Rouge. I think that was my first time that I realized that 'one hand extended can make a difference.'"

Judy knows that life is really all the little things that happen day by day and how they add up. The little ways we help others and others help us make up the joy of life. And it is the exemplification of legacy. Our legacy is in moments and actions, day by day. She shares, "By the time I was in high school, my parents started having financial troubles. My dad's furniture business was not doing well; it was located in a downtrodden area. My parents had kids in high school and college, and they didn't know how they were going to keep me in my girls' Catholic high school in uptown New Orleans, St. Mary's Dominican School. My aunt, Dorothy Weber, said that I was not going to leave Dominican— that she would pay my tuition for my final two years so I could graduate from Dominican. She said she believed in me. That was a gift for which I will be forever grateful—both for her generosity and her faith in me. It meant so much."

"Each of these little things I saw people do, whether they were my parents, my brother, my aunt or people around me, influenced me. I transferred to the University of New Orleans after three semesters at LSU and was about to graduate in business school with a BS in marketing. I was asked by my business law teacher to stay after the class one day. I thought maybe I was in trouble. He suggested to me that I should go to law school. Again, that was somebody taking the time to reach out to somebody else and say, 'You can do this. I believe in you. I want to invest in you.'"

The importance of older lawyers mentoring young lawyers is not lost on Judy. She says, "For instance, in my twenty-one years of private practice, as well as my dozen years in-house, and now, I take the time to go to lunch with young lawyers to keep in touch with them, to mentor them in both in formal and informal settings. Within my company law department, I spend a lot of time talking to young lawyers about how they can get involved, in the bar or *pro bono*, if they choose. It may not be for everybody but it is worth a try by everyone. The last several years when I have spoken at Tulane Law School at their freshman orientation day on professionalism, I tell them why I think it's so beneficial for them to get involved from early on, and the many ways in which they can get involved in bar associations and in public service work. Mentoring is a very important part of what I believe lawyers have an obligation to do. It keeps our professional values and obligation to serve the public front and center by making sure we talk with young lawyers about how important it is to contribute to our profession and the public. Young lawyers are so appreciative of the fact that you spend time with them, whether it's over a cup of coffee or lunch, and you can tell that they look forward to their chance to learn more about how they can get involved."

In addition to her family life, Judy remembers one critically defining moment that influenced her, and shaped her to be the lawyer and individual she is today. In her first semester of law school, she signed up to attend a panel on post-conviction capital habeas cases representation. "I recall that the one panelist who struck me the most was a gentleman by the name of Sam Dalton, who was a criminal defense attorney in New Orleans. He had handled multiple capital cases as well as appeals and postconviction habeas proceedings in both state and federal courts. I listened to him and realized that as important as what lawyers do in terms of representing, advising, and counseling individual and corporate clients in every area of commercial law and civil law in general law, it is also important to lend oneself to indigent representation in criminal matters, if possible, at least at some point in your career, because the need is so great. Sam gave a gift, and he got a gift in return, as I understood his message, because he believed representing indigent clients in criminal matters, particularly capital cases, was the essence of lawyering. He struck me as somebody who made the case for advocacy and meaningful representation better than anybody I have ever heard."

Years later, when Judy had started practicing, her firm was asked to take on a capital habeas representation and the firm asked Judy to take the case. Along with a partner and dear friend, Denise Puente, represented John Ashley Brown, Jr. on death row in Louisiana for nine years. She remembers him as a very grateful client and says, "He worked with us and despite help from a whole team of people we were not able to save him from execution." Denise and Judy did a tremendous amount of work on the case along with a team of paralegals, secretaries, and other experienced capital habeas lawyers who contributed their resources and their talent. She says with emotion in her voice, "Denise and I were there the night that John Ashley Brown was executed. John got the representation, or at least I hope he did, that Sam Dalton said we should give. In that way, John gave us a gift in allowing us to give ourselves."

Since attending that panel at law school, Judy took the importance of representation to heart and it stays with her to this day. I asked how the representation of John Ashley Brown, Jr. changed her. "It changes you as an individual and as a lawyer and as a citizen. You realize that you can always find redeeming qualities about a human being no matter what had happened in the past. We should all live and believe in redemption. I could not square the person I had come to know and represent with the person that the state was going to put to death. I thought about the dignity of a person who probably had not felt dignity before in his life; as he walked from where he lived in a holding cell to the execution room, John stood tall; even as several of the guards and the warden wiped away their tears. I can't imagine what was going through John's mind but seeing him that night made me realize, with the greatest enduring respect for the victim and her family and their loss, that my representation of John had been a blessing in my life and would always be."

To this day, Judy strives to always be her best, and give that highest level of representation. However, she recognizes it may still not be enough. "You can never fall short of doing your best or do less, because once you have given your best and your all, and it didn't work, you will always strive to give your best and your all, each and every time."

Judy keeps the last warrant of death decision by the Supreme Court on the John Ashley Brown case with her in her home office. She says, "This order keeps me grounded about what's important in life and what's important in my professional career. It serves as a reminder that you work very hard as a lawyer, yet you don't always succeed, but that doesn't mean that you weren't doing the absolute best that you could do for your client. It means no matter what you think will be your best, you have to do more."

One thing Judy said truly resonated with me: "There is an ache in you as a lawyer to help people. I think that is what sets the profession of law apart from a lot of other wonderful contributing professions. It is a desire to speak for the people who cannot speak for themselves. It is a desire to make sure that people understand what we understand about our democracy and our systems of government and about our justice system and the rule of law particularly. If we, the lawyers, are not vocal about what we have of value to preserve, then how can we expect the regular layperson that is not trained in law to appreciate and value the greatness of our country?"

# Be Just and Fair to Everyone

*Mark Lane*

The late Mark Lane considered the day he was born to be his first defining moment. In our conversation together, he spent a great deal of time recounting the blessing of having a mother and father who, in his words, "by their actions, not their lectures, told us what was fair and what should be done." He regards both his parents as extraordinary people who instilled in him and his siblings that it is imperative to "be just and fair to everyone." Mark thought about his parents' lessons in fairness throughout his life, and how those lessons shaped and cemented his vision of justice.

Mark grew up in Brooklyn in the 1920s, when the borough was still predominantly white and a far cry from the diverse neighborhood it is today. One of his earliest encounters with diversity came when he was a young boy and a neighbor hired a maid. His mother inquired as to how much the friend would be paying the maid, who was a woman of color, and Mark was shocked when he heard his mother's friend respond, "Well, I'm going to tell her that after she finishes the day's work." Mark realized that, "regardless of what her wages should be, the maid would have no choice but to accept it." His mother's disappointment in her friend reinforced Mark's gut feeling, even at his young age, that this was an unfair situation, and this seemingly innocuous interaction stayed with him for more than eighty years.

After graduating, Mark opened his first office in East Harlem which, at the time, was one of the most depressed areas in New York City. Even then, he often thought back to his youth and his parents telling him what was fair and what was not. I asked whether his first cases came to him, or if he sought them out. He told me about the nearby "slums in Bombay, six-story tenements that were inexpensive in those days, but not if you didn't have any money." Three families would live in one small apartment, splitting the day eight hours each way. When their eight hours were up, the family would take to the street until their turn came around again.

Mark knew what he was getting into opening his office in this area. However, he was still somewhat surprised when he realized he would have almost no say in who made up his clientele—those who lived nearby would walk in and decide he was going to be their lawyer. He told me, "If they had any money to pay me that was a good thing, because I had to rent to pay."

But what about those who couldn't pay? As Mark remembers, this was the case most of the time. He once tried a three-week case with a young kid who was charged with murder. The kid didn't do it. Mark was paid $50.

But even paying rent didn't deter Mark from finding justice for everyone—especially underrepresented minorities. He continued to take on primarily criminal cases, and his first year quickly turned into ten. "Those ten years in East Harlem were the most rewarding part of my life."

Mark was still working out of his storefront office in East Harlem during the 1960s when Mayor Carmine DeSapio brought about a brief resurgence of the Tammany Hall political machine. Rather than standing idly by, Mark took the bull by the horns and helped found the Reform Democrat movement within the New York Democratic Party. He ran against a Democratic incumbent for a seat in the New York State Assembly. During his campaign, he endured death threats and "things like that," but he won. On his success, he said "I won the primary, by and large, by going at them like a sound track every day and urging people to register to vote. People in the neighborhood, mostly Puerto Ricans, who had lived there for fifty years, had never registered, but they registered during our campaign."

I likened his run to a modern-day grass roots campaign. He agreed, but quipped, "Yeah, we don't have a lot of grass in East Harlem." But he acknowledged his success came down to the people he had been helping in years prior. "The winner was decided by the people in the neighborhood, and that's where I won," he said. During his campaign, he told the people in Harlem Yorkville that, "I would be their voice in the State Legislation and the voice of the people of the State of New York, but I would not be the voice of the Democratic Party, I would not be the voice of organized crime, and I would not be the voice of Carmine DeSapio."

Unsurprisingly, he stayed true to his word. At the time of his term, the state legislature was run by a caucus system. Rather than having formal caucuses among the parties, according to Mark, there would simply be a meeting of Democrats and someone would say "Okay, this is a caucus now," and a discussion would follow. Party leadership would make a decision, and everyone else would follow suit. Never one to stick by the status quo, Mark made it clear from day one that he would not be falling in line.

"When I got there, I said, 'Mr. Speaker, would you tell me when this becomes a caucus?' He said, 'Why?' I said, 'Because I will not attend any caucus.'" He promised then and there that he would walk out as soon as it became a caucus. The media picked up on it and were soon waiting right outside the assembly room waiting for Mark to walk out. However, they never had a caucus. "For the first time in the history of the Democratic Party, the New York State legislature did not have a caucus. Not one in the two years I was there, because they knew I would go out if there was a caucus."

Growing up, his mother had a picture of one of his friends, Eleanor Roosevelt, on the wall. It's no secret that Eleanor Roosevelt took Mark under her wing during his early campaigns. He remembers his mother saying, "Isn't she beautiful?" Mark says, "Well, she wasn't beautiful in the Marilyn Monroe sense, but she was a very beautiful person, and you could see that." They originally met when Eleanor called Mark asking how she could help on his campaign. She told him, "I know you need funds. I will host a little fund-raising luncheon at my house."

As all good sons would do, Mark immediately called his mother and relayed the news that Eleanor Roosevelt had invited him to a luncheon at her house. "My mother said, 'Oh you will have to tell me everything that happens.' I said, 'I'm not going to tell you what happened—you're going to be there.'" Mark's mother sat next to Eleanor at the luncheon.

Mark loves animals and tells me, "If you have a dog, you live longer. I'll tell you that." In many ways, Mark seems to only consist of his tough exterior. He fought the machine; he won. He fought against racism, unfairness, prejudice, poverty, and he came out for the better. But as most lawyers do, Mark has his soft spot. In Mark's case, "Her name was Giselle."

Mark and his wife adopted Giselle as a nine-week-old German Shepherd puppy. But Giselle was more than just a pet. Mark wrote a children's book about her. At the time of our interview, Giselle had passed, but as Mark told me, "She is still in my heart every day." After raising a dog with a clear impact on his life, Mark thought he would be a one-time dog owner, but his wife of many years convinced him otherwise. She looked at a website for abused rescued dogs and found a German Shepherd, all black, smaller than most, who had been abused for a year. They decided to adopt a rescue dog. "It's been a great, rewarding experience." Her name is Juliette, and he and his wife rarely say no to her.

I asked Mark what advice he would give to a group of law students about entering the profession. He said he didn't have advice because, "Everybody has a different standard of success." But he wanted to make it clear: "Law is unfair. It's unfair now just as it was a long time ago. The law says that neither rich people nor poor people can sleep on the subway. But we know what that means. Rich people don't have to do that."

He does advise, "If you go to law school because you want to try to change things, make the law responsive to ordinary people. See it as a tool on behalf of the people, not some old statute somewhere. Then I think it is worthwhile. Then if you have any other idea about what the law is about, go ahead, but you don't get a pat on the back from it."

# Lift Others as You Climb

*Hon. Pamila J. Brown*

Born the child of schoolteachers in Bel Air, Maryland, a small town with segregated schools, Pamila was "one of four brown kids" at her newly-integrated elementary school. Her early defining moments were the sting of an unjustified bias that had nothing to do with anything but the color of her skin. For example, her second-grade teacher would fix everyone's hair but hers. She says, "At recess all the little girls would play and sometimes your braids would come undone or your ribbon would come out. She would always re-braid my friend's hair, but she would not re-braid mine. If my braid came out and I asked her to put my ribbon back in, she said, 'Your mother will have to do it.'"

When she asked for help with math, the teacher would pat her on the head and tell her not to worry about it, that "all little colored kids have trouble with math." The experience instilled in her the understanding of the "power of our words." She says, "Second grade had a profound effect on me the rest of my life. I always struggled with math. As a result, I never told my mom about it until I was in junior high school. Because of that experience, I refrained from calling people names and knew that when our parents said the saying 'sticks and stones may break my bones, but words will never hurt me,' for the parents of children of color, they said it to protect us, to give us a sense of balance."

Things got a little better for her because she was a good student and had a wonderful fourth-grade teacher, Mrs. Fitzgerald. She was in fourth grade when President Kennedy was shot and she remembers the class stopping. She got the best grades in that class. Mrs. Fitzgerald inspired her to do well in school. But the prejudice continued in her life and it was evident everywhere. She says, "Then you go to high school and, as I said, our town was segregated, there was a lunch counter at the drugstore. We went in there, but you weren't supposed to sit at the counter. Then the movie theater, the blacks were forced to go through the side stairs. When we were little, we would never go to the movies in Bel Air. We would always go into Baltimore City because the movie theaters were integrated then." These early experiences shaped her sense of justice and formed her sense of fairness to all people, regardless of their race or color.

One of her first defining moments occurred when Black Panther H. Rap Brown was tried for incitement and weapons violations in the wake of the riots following the assassination of Martin Luther King, Jr. Then a high school student, Pamila was determined to see the trial. She says, "I snuck in, but I was not able to get very far. I did get to see William Kunstler, the defense attorney, and, honestly, with his suit and tie and disheveled hair, he looked like a wild man."

"William Kunstler was a very famous lawyer, and it just so happened that I got to see him again at work when I was in college because he was the lawyer representing Russell Means in the Wounded Knee trials, which were moved from the Dakotas to Minnesota where the federal district court was." Judge Brown first had the thought that she wanted to be a lawyer when she saw this man who "took a risk of representing this African American man at a time when the riots were going on. He wasn't going to be very popular. But he was going to use the law to defend H. Rap Brown."

At that time, like so many other female interviewees in this book, when she went to the guidance office, they would all suggest being a teacher or a social worker. She says, "Nobody encouraged me to be a lawyer. I assume because they didn't know any black lawyers, and they were trying to be responsible. My parents said, 'You can do whatever you want to do.' They always did that. Every sort of challenge, they were always there and very supportive."

Her next defining moment opened her up in new ways and prepared her for the path that was to come. It was the summer between high school and college. She went to Nairobi, Kenya, in Africa on a Girl Scout trip called the Jubilee where out of 10,000 applicants, she was one of four picked. Minion Cameron was her Girl Scout leader and her husband was a lawyer who became a judge. During that three-month summer trip, they went on a safari, stayed two weeks with an African family, toured for two weeks and participated in the two-week Jubilee. This was before the television show *Roots* came out. She says, "I think every African American who saw *Roots* was profoundly affected by it. I don't know of a person of my age who did not sit and watch all of the series of *Roots* when it first came out. It was eye-opening. But during my Africa trip, I actually ran in this grassy plain and fell in the tall grass and began to cry and thought, 'This is where I came from.' The two African guides assigned to us yelled at me to come back because they were afraid of lions. Africa is mostly wide, expansive plains and mountains. That's where the lions are—in the plains. That was just a breathtaking thing. It was something I did on a whim as an impetuous eighteen-year-old girl. It was overpowering. I did not know about *Roots*; I had not gone to college; I didn't know any of those historical things. I just got a sense of freedom that I will never forget."

Pamila remembers that she was a "bit rebellious" on this trip when she was interviewed by a newspaper in Nairobi and with a bandana and a flower in her hair. She recalls, "I was not supposed to talk to the press. I was not supposed to be outside without my Girl Scout uniform. I was asked what I thought about the United States boycotting the Olympics if South Africa was going to be participating. My father was an Olympian—he was in the Pan American Games. I knew how I felt about apartheid, and I said the US should not participate in a country that practices apartheid. Unbeknownst to me, President Nixon had already said that the United States was participating in the games and that the games should not be political. The little contract I signed before I went on the trip, which I never read, said that I was supposed to be in uniform in public, which does not include a bandana and a flower; that I was not supposed to speak publicly about anything that was political; and I was not supposed to speak against US policy."

At that time, Pamila was going to try and "change the world and make it a better place." What she saw in Africa, the abject poverty she had never seen before, changed her. That's when Idi Amin was in power and she says, "I went away to school and I got more enlightened and then Attica happened while I was at school."

Her first experience of real diversity was in St. Paul, Minnesota, at Macalester College. Around that time, the Attica prison riot in

New York, where all these inmates were killed, happened. She remembers, "I had wonderful political science professors and I really excelled in college. I was very active in student government. We actually took over a building because they were going to cut the financial aid to students of color. I don't remember how long we were in this building, but they had a federal mediator come in. My parents were just beside themselves because by that time, my freshman year, I had already decided I really wanted to go to law school. They were like, 'Well, you're not going to go to law school if you get arrested.' We did not get arrested; we didn't do anything to the building. It was a peaceful demonstration. We occupied the building, and it made the news in the Twin Cities."

The school restored part of the funding, which led to another of her defining moments. She asked herself whether she should leave the school because she says, "I was risking my whole future to take a stand to make a point. It is so funny because every time I get the alumni magazine, ironically one of the people who protested with me is on the Alumni Board of Advisors and I was given the Outstanding Alumni award by the school."

Pamila had another chance to protest while she was in law school. She says, "I went to law school in 1976 and there was only one other woman of color in my law school freshman class. My class was probably 20 percent women. I remember we were fighting about the Women's Law Student Association because we had to go to the bathroom on the third floor and there were no women's bathrooms on the classroom floors, no 'potty parity'; thus, women were historically late to class because if they went to the restroom, they couldn't get to class on time. We fought for that and now it's just so remarkable that now there are so many women in law school."

Getting to be a judge in Baltimore was not the easiest path for Pamila, but her sheer determination helped her keep trying until she succeeded. She shares, "It was really a struggle to get here. We have a judicial selection committee called the Trial Courts Nominating Commission. The commissioners are individuals appointed by the governor. They interview the candidates and decide which names go up to the governor for selection. I actually made the list four separate times before being appointed. You can imagine, each time it was very disheartening to not get selected. I remember the last time, I was just giving it every ounce of me, I said to myself, 'I'm not leaving any stone unturned. I'm speaking to everybody.' It was hard because I'm really outgoing, I'm real gregarious, but if you ask me to sit and talk about myself, I don't do that comfortably. But in this system, you have got to be saying, 'I'm the best thing since sliced bread. I am the candidate. I've been a litigator for over twenty years. I've done this, I've done that, etc.' It's tooting your own horn, and even though you have all these other advocates doing it for you, it is important that you have the comfort level to be able to do that."

Pamila has created legacy all along the path of her life, from being active in student government in college and in law school to becoming the first woman and the first person of color to serve as president of the Student Bar Association at the University of Baltimore School of Law. She became the first black woman president of the Baltimore City Bar Association and the Maryland Bar Association. She recalls an early ABA speech "about the learned professions—law, medicine, and religion—and that even as through each of those you are making a living by doing what you do, you're also making a difference by serving the public in some way." She says, "That always stuck with me."

Pamila has led an exciting life and has left a legacy of her own. You create legacy with every step you take up the ladder of success.

# Stretch Yourself

*Karen J. Mathis*

"I'm an Army brat. My family has four generations of military service, and I was born to a young man in the Air Force and my mother in Providence, Rhode Island. I have three younger sisters. I was brought up going to eight schools in the first eight years of my schooling." At the age of twelve, Karen thought she was going to grow up to be a nun, because "nuns were the most independent, educated women I knew."

Karen is very self-directed and says, "The three strong influences in my life were a close-knit family, the nuns who educated me and believed in noblesse oblige, and the military tradition of honor and service to country. All three of those things were very important because they helped form my view of the world and service to others to always be willing to give a person a chance no matter what their background was."

Growing up in Rhode Island in the 1950s, there weren't many opportunities afforded to women. You could be a home-maker, a teacher, a nurse, or a nun. Those are the memories of my youth.

However, Karen defied the odds. "There were no lawyers in my family. In fact, I was the first person in my family to go to college, let alone graduate school. I had a strong mother who felt that education was important." From a young age, education was a major priority for her. "That was always in the back of my mind. If you want a profession, you've got to have something to fall back on." However, it wasn't until her teenage years, after her parents divorced, that she realized she wanted to be a lawyer.

Coming from a Catholic upbringing, divorce was an unfamiliar subject to the Mathis family. When her father became involved with someone else, her mother was left to seek out a divorce lawyer, a time Karen remembers being very difficult for her whole family. "I remember that lawyer being a real helping person. I think my mother paid him off, and I'm not kidding about this, at $5 a week for about four years. Without his help, I don't know what would have happened to our family." As it turned out, some years passed, and her mother did remarry a wonderful man and they were married until his death.

Karen worked and got a scholarship to get through both college and law school. She says, "I received scholarships to both the University of Denver and the University of Colorado School of Law. I worked all the way through college and always had at least one job, sometimes two. It was the same thing in law school. I had three younger sisters at home, and I lived at home during the summer, but my parents were not able to give me financial support for school." Once she reached law school, Karen knew she had found her people. "I loved law school. I loved the intellectual curiosity of it." Karen's time in law school was also the beginning of a series of impressive, if not surprising, firsts for her.

First, Karen said yes to trying out for the University of Colorado women's basketball team. A friend of hers suggested it shortly after the National Collegiate Athletic Association sanctioned women's basketball. Despite being graduate students, they still had eligibility. She says, "Like a couple of idiots, we went out for the varsity basketball team at the University of Colorado and we made the team." Unfortunately (or fortunately in Karen's opinion), that same year the Big Eight league mandated that any league games in which graduate students played in would automatically be forfeited. Karen recalls the coach approaching her and telling her she was "on the team fair and square, 'but if you stay on the team, we'll lose the game.'" Karen graciously left the team and continued to pursue her education.

Between her first and second year of law school, Karen worked for the Army JAG in Colorado Springs, where she served under the student exemption as a legal assistance lawyer for military men and their families. "This was the summer of 1973, and at that time they had a policy in the US Army that if you were defense counsel, you had to be the most senior counsel they had. The best people would be defense counsel in military justice." Although she was a civilian, wearing civilian clothes, during her first week a captain came in and called her Captain Mathis—because all JAGs are captains. Her second week, a major came in and called her Major Mathis. An unusual situation for any law student, but Karen took it in stride. "I went to the Staff Judge Advocate and I said kiddingly, 'Well sir, if you'll make me a Lieutenant Colonel, I'll sign up.'"

The next summer, Karen worked for the US Army in Germany. Karen was in Germany for four months. She worked with young service men coming back from Vietnam, many of whom were minorities. At twenty-three years old, Karen was sitting second chair to capital murder cases, kidnapping, and drug charges. "By the time I got out of law school, it was like, 'What's the big deal about going into court?'"

But upon graduation, Karen took a very unexpected route, again stretching herself to new heights. She went to work for what is now KPMG as a tax lawyer and was "the first woman they had ever hired in Denver in the tax department." The hiring manager took her to the Petroleum Club, only to find out that because she was a woman she wouldn't be allowed to enter. "We had to sit in the lobby next to the reception desk and have tea."

"It's a great way to give back. If a person becomes a lawyer, he or she should give back, to their individual clients, to their communities, and to their profession." Karen was the first vice president of the Colorado Bar, the second woman president of the Colorado Young Lawyers, and went on to become president of the American Bar Association where she created the Youth at Risk Program and many other successful programs. "Bar work gives you an opportunity, not just to do the work you can do, but to mobilize others with your vision of giving back. That is what is in it for me."

Even as a seasoned attorney, Karen is not one to slow down. After her immediate past presidency year in the ABA in 2008, she moved to Prague, Czech Republic, accepting an offer to become the executive director of the CEELI Institute. "I rented an apartment that I had never seen, worked in a country where I did not know two words of the language, and took a sabbatical from my law firm for a year." While there, Karen was recruited to become president and CEO of Big Brothers and Big Sisters. "We mentored a quarter of a million children one-on-one every year." In 2012, Karen returned to Denver where she became the Associate Executive Director of the Institute for the Advancement of the American Legal System at the University of Denver. She retired from that position in 2018. However, she says she hasn't fully retired, but rather "rewired," and she is continuing her international rule of law work and work with children. "Perhaps it is my third session of service."

One thing that struck me during my conversation with Karen is that she rarely, if ever, says no. Karen took a multitude of chances throughout her life, and the rewards to both her and our community as lawyers are obvious. "At the end of your life, people are going to ask you how much good did you do? Today is the beginning of your life when you're going to be writing that story. Be sure that at the end of your life, you're happy with the way that story reads."

# Just Do It

*Laurel G. Bellows*

Laurel is an only child raised by her mother, grandmother, and aunt; all were big influences in her life. Laurel's mother supported their small family by doing "dramatic reading." Laurel says, "She would take a book and turn it into a dramatic reading and then do a one-person show." Laurel's mother grew up with food rations during the depression and was extremely careful about money. "There was no waste in our house."

Laurel's grandmother, a concert pianist, lived only a few blocks away and played an important part in her upbringing, teaching Laurel to play piano as early as four years old. "Quite a bit of my upbringing was being surrounded by her. She was an amazing, beautiful, kind, and gentle woman. She was small and chubby with this angelic face and you would think only of her kindness until she sat down at the piano and pounded out Rachmaninoff. The whole world changed just in that moment and she was able to express herself. The piano made her powerful . . . a force to be reckoned with. But then I lost her when I was eleven."

Laurel learned independence from her grandmother's sister, her great aunt, Beatrice Newmark. "She was a very, very independent woman. Her passport was issued in the late 1800s initially, and she traveled the world on her own." Laurel's great aunt was never married, preferring to be self-sustaining. She ran the family's jewelry store for years.

Growing up in such a matriarchal family, I wondered if Laurel learned to support other women in her youth. "Growing up, the importance of supporting women was never on my priority list. Instead, my mom preached the imperative of economic independence. I grew up in the law in the age of 'don't be a woman, be a lawyer.' The message was 'be a good lawyer and just by chance be a woman,' as opposed to 'be a great woman who happens to be a lawyer.'"

Laurel graduated from law school in 1974, during a time when it was best to blend into the man's world. "When I became president of the Chicago Bar in 1991–1992, I looked around; I saw women judges, not many, of course; there were women practicing law in big firms and in small firms like the firm I chose, but women trial lawyers were rare." Laurel wanted to use her time as president of the Chicago Bar to take stock of how women were faring in the profession. She invited five close friends to a breakfast to discuss the issues and successes women were seeing in their industry. She arrived to find seventy women. "I realized at that moment that things were not good, that women were not doing well, and that we needed to openly address the status of women in the legal profession."

That day, a quarter of a century ago, was a defining moment of Laurel's life confronting the inequality suffered by women lawyers. On that day, the celebrated Chicago Bar Association Alliance for Women was founded.

While Laurel was tackling women's issues in a big way, she was also facing them in her own career. She wanted to be a trial lawyer, but couldn't find any firms that were hiring women to try cases, so she called up her alma mater, Loyola University, to ask for guidance. She was pointed in the direction of a man with a small firm, only two attorneys, who was looking to hire specifically a woman to train to try cases. Apparently, he had good reasons. He said, "Women build relationships very quickly, it's what they are about. If a woman stands in front of a jury of six or twelve people a woman can build a relationship in two minutes; the jury will trust her." He was also brutally honest with Laurel. "He said, 'You know what? You won't leave me. No woman, particularly a woman trial lawyer, is going to leave me and steal my clients and open her own firm and try cases because she won't be able to eat. Nobody will hire her.' And guess what? He was right." This man became her husband and partner in life.

Even once she had a job, being a trial lawyer was still a challenge. Every morning in Chicago, every lawyer that had a trial on call would congregate in one courtroom. "You have three to four hundred lawyers every single morning in the courtroom where the chief judge would send out cases. There were no women attorneys present. You would walk into a courtroom of all men—absolutely no women." The judge often confused her for a student, secretary, or law clerk. Laurel recalls, "A man would say, 'Hey, honey, what case is this? You send your lawyer in here.' She would respond, 'I am the lawyer.' He would say, 'No, come on. You're kidding, honey. You're not trying this case.'" She says, "My reaction was part pride, fear, and humiliation that so many women went through. It's a reality we lived with and we don't communicate to our young women thoroughly enough today." Through all of the hardships, Laurel persevered and fought for her dream. She quotes her favorite Chinese proverb that helped her through the rough times: "The person who says it cannot be done should not interrupt the person doing it."

From an early age, Laurel was defined by the way people saw her, and allowed that to become her own definition of herself. "Small, just this little person, a little quiet person, kind of non-descript, not pretty, not special to anybody else, except maybe my mom. That is how I saw myself for so many years. There is a big part of me that remains small, then there is a big part of me that, as a result of being small and always feeling that I had to prove myself. That big inner part of me is something that I carry with me all the time. Now I know how to use being small."

Although Laurel may at times feel physically small, she has fought and conquered feelings of insignificance. "I just took these issues on determined to define myself by what I do, and do it well, so that what I accomplish will be icing on the cake. I think many women think the same way." She found ways to distinguish herself from her taller, male colleagues. "The only way I can do that is to do something very, very different, something strong, something the men would have never had the need or the courage to do . . . And, just get it done."

When discussing the National Council of Bar presidents, Laurel said, "In one defining moment you could actually change the universe in a certain area because you sent three hundred and fifty bar leaders out into the world with a program they wanted to run. I would say to myself, 'This is power.' Power used well. This is a platform. Imagine what one person can do. Create a program to answer a need. Run a program to revamp Juvenile Justice in Chicago. Then showcase it at the National Council of Bar Presidents. And the world changes. It's pretty amazing to inspire state bar and metropolitan bar leaders to change their corner of the world—all of the sudden, the law and policy of our country regarding juveniles' changes." Now Laurel is focused on eradicating modern-day slavery in our country.

Laurel takes risks. "I never wore the dark suits, I never wore that tiny little tie, I never tried to dress like the guys. I've always dressed in bold colors, I always distinguished myself to make certain there was no doubt that I am a woman. I am a woman, a lawyer, and an advocate for equality and freedom. Like I say, just do it!"

# Integrate Faith into Action

*Dr. Artika R. Tyner*

---

Artika is a lawyer, author, and educator. She tapped into her purpose early in her career and tells us in her TEDx talk that she discovered that she is a "freedom fighter with an Afro." Her passion and integrity stand out in all she does. She is a strong, yet passionate leader who is an inspiration to all.

Artika is fourth generation out of Minnesota's Twin Cities area, and she grew up in the era of the war on drugs and violence. She says, "It was definitely a decade of turmoil for the African American community. If you looked at the intersection of race and poverty and the immigrant population, you would see turmoil. I had a community-based upbringing. It takes a village to raise a child."

One of her defining moments as a child was realizing that her library card was her passport to the world. She remarks, "I was real close friends with my doll, but that meant that I had a lot of time in isolation because I was so much younger than my siblings—they were teenagers, and I was a small child. I spent a lot of time studying and researching. For me, my library card was my highway to the world. I got to experience all of the places I could visit someday. Reading and writing was my tool for processing the world around me and offered me a great insight into the possibilities for my future."

Artika's grandmother, Nellie Lightfoot, gave her a sense of the importance of having a purpose in life and taught her to take a stand with the tools she possessed. She shares, "Her tools were cooking, warm hospitality; she had a heart of direct servitude." Her grandmother had high goals for Artika, and, as a result, Artika became the first-generation college graduate and law school graduate in her family. She believes she was groomed by her grandmother early on to become the leader she is today.

Law school was a way for Artika to achieve the next step of living out her goal to provide service and commitment to her community. She says, "I knew that if I became a lawyer, I would be more empowered to make the changes that were needed, whether it was access to a better education or understanding and navigating the criminal justice system. In college, it was just a question of which tools I would gain to help me achieve my goals in law school."

Artika is already thinking of her legacy, and her goal is to have a "sense of knowing that I used the gifts and talents that I have in my own way." Her mother, Jacklyn Milton, who, like her grandmother, is a very important influence in her life, admonished her, "Be the best original. Be yourself." As a result of following her mother's advice, Dr. Tyner serves as a voice for the voiceless. As a professor, she encourages her students to be "social engineers." She pushes them to pull up their sleeves and say, "How can I get involved to make a difference?" Her living legacy now is seeing her students go out and make an impact on the world.

Artika loves being a part of her community. She loves to go into the grocery store and talk to people about the plights they are facing and to think strategically about how she can help make a difference in their lives. She recognizes her gift is her ability to see the larger issues and problem solve around them for better solutions. Artika wrote her dissertation on "Lawyers as Leaders." She was passionate about learning about lawyers who engage in the social change movement and identifying their leadership characteristics and the tools they use to build social change. She read *The Souls of Black Folk* by W.E.B. Du Bois, and, although the book is more than one hundred years old, it felt to her as if it had been written today. It was a divine connection, and she decided to get her doctoral decree so that she could help her community interact with the world in a new way. She wanted to use her legal training and her policy training to help bring forward social policy changes.

A real defining moment for Artika was when she went to the Mississippi Center for Justice. At that time, she thought the civil rights movement was over. But her eyes were opened in Mississippi. She saw a lot of unfinished business in terms of the fact that "we had not advanced much since the Emancipation Proclamation." She saw firsthand that there were a lot of young people unemployed and just hopeless. She says, "I feel like I have to play a key role in making sure that the future does not unfold in the way it has in the past."

I asked Artika to explain what she meant by her LEAD line about faith and she said, "I think my faith influences how I look at the world. My faith is a personal relationship with Jesus Christ first and foremost. I grew up Pentecostal with some Baptist influences. My grandfather was Catholic. Therefore, I had a good mixture of backgrounds to draw from, and I took the pearls of wisdom from each tradition."

Artika talks about her social justice advocacy. "It's not an easy task to raise controversial or challenging issues, but still I think it has to be done. That's why I say faith plays a role because, of course, I might get discouraged, become overwhelmed, and someday might say I want to quit. But I think faith steps in to tell me that I have the grace to do it, that God is with me to do it, and that he will give me the words to say and instruct me in the process. That is why I say I couldn't do it without faith. It is a process of renewal, and I think it's also a process of instruction, because faith is one of the values that I believe in."

Another benefit of integrating your faith into your actions is the fact that you know that you "are not walking alone" she says. "There are also others in your faith community who can support you and walk with you." Artika asks her students, "What is in your hands? What is in your sphere of influence to make a difference in the world? Everybody has something, but I think the worst-case scenario in life is to do nothing at all and just stay on the sidelines."

Artika, like me, stuttered as a child. She said, "I think it was when I was nervous. I joked about it and said it was because my thoughts were coming out faster than my words. With speech therapy I learned a lot, but as an adult it is always in the back of my mind. In the beginning of my career, I tried to stay behind the scenes and thought I might just do transactional law. But as life unfolded, I was pushed out of my comfort zone. At first, I was truly nervous, like I think I was still stuttering back then, even when I first started practicing law. Then I just felt like God would be my voice. He would give me the words to speak and give me the confidence to do it. I think once I found and connected myself to the issues I was passionate about, the rest was history. I tell that story to my students. Wherever they are, whatever they are doing, they can overcome the odds if they are doing something and put their whole heart into it."

Artika laughs when she remarks that most people would never believe how shy and quiet she was until she found her voice and purpose and pushed forward—they are thinking that she is never quiet now! Artika is a perfect example of someone who started out thinking one way and then really tapped into her life purpose and used her faith as fuel to accomplish her goals. We can all learn a lot from her wisdom. We both share the belief that our faith drives our careers. We feel it is woven into the tapestry of our lives—both professional and personal—and we can't discuss one aspect without discussing the other. By knowing who she is and what her purpose is, she is able to create her life and career accordingly.

# Lead a Productive Life of Public Service

*Sandy D'Alemberte*

Sandy was born in Tallahassee, Florida, in 1933 in an old house that was directly across the street on the western side of the State Capitol. It was in the days before air conditioning where you could sit in a rocker on his grandmother's front porch and actually hear people debating legislature. His great uncle was a Florida Supreme Court justice and his house was on the other side of the Capitol.

In those days, there were old houses on all sides of the Capitol. It was a wonderful playground. The Capitol was very much a part of his life. His father became a lawyer in the middle of the Depression and it was the segregated South, but he worked as the purchasing agent for the state institution.

Sandy went to all white schools in Chattahoochee, Florida, fifty miles to the west. There, he remembers fondly, "There were many acres of well-maintained, beautiful green expanses that were great to play in during the daytime and as night fell, especially in the summer months, you'd see fireflies everywhere. It's one of those great mystical things in my memory to think back on how many fireflies you would see—flying like sparks over the grassy areas."

Sandy's father went into the service during WWII and he says, "WWII is really a critical part of my understanding of the world. First of all, I lived both in the North and the South during this period of time. The South, of course, was thoroughly segregated; the North was not. I think my understanding of WWII may have been deeper than most people's understanding of it, partly because we were dealing with countries that were in some respect a maze to us. Our troops were stationed in England, we were fighting with Germany, we were dealing in parts of the world we hardly understood, but we were blessed to have leaders who could actually explain why we were at war. Think back on the speeches of Roosevelt and of Churchill. Think how important it was for your understanding to have a president or prime minister who were so articulate and who could explain to you what was happening in the war and why we were at war. I think people who lived through WWII had the benefit of that remarkable leadership. That leadership was largely missing during the Vietnam War. Roosevelt articulated the Four Freedoms: The freedom from fear, freedom from want, freedom of speech, and freedom of religion and thought. Those were principles. They were spoken of in ways that were connected to the war effort. They were thinking about the basics."

These early experiences formed the basics of Sandy's life work. He decided early on, by the time he was a junior in high school, that "segregation was wrong. I thought it was stupid." He went to the University of the South, or Sewanee, with a scholarship. Then he went to graduate school after serving in the Navy. He went to the London School of Economics for a year and then went to the University of Florida to law school. He says, "I was hired by an old-line Florida firm; a firm that had been established back in the 1920s, and it had a number of incarnations, but it was originally organized by Scott Loftin who was a president of the American Bar Association, and for a short time, a United States senator." He represented big clients like National Airlines, which merged into Pan American Airlines. He also represented the *Miami Herald* and Florida Power & Light.

Sandy's commitment to racial equality continued during his career. He remembers, "Florida had a great governor named LeRoy Collins. He successfully integrated Florida. When he ran for Senate he lost in part because of his efforts to integrate. I realized that LeRoy Collins is by far the greatest Florida leader that I've known, in part because he had the courage to deal with that issue in a way that it should have been dealt with, and he led Florida through that period of time without any great violence. But he stuck to principle."

Sandy was the Florida campaign manager for Bob Kennedy in 1968 but "Of course, we never got to run a campaign because he was assassinated before we had our primary. The primary was in September and he was assassinated in June of 1968. That left me discouraged about political life and made me withdraw from national politics."

But not for long. When the McGovern campaign came along in '72, George McGovern asked him to be his Florida campaign manager. He agreed and realized that, "I was associated with a man very much like Governor LeRoy Collins, who was highly principled and who might not succeed. He did not succeed in becoming president but did succeed with joining together the forces that brought Nixon around to ending the Vietnam War. George McGovern was a very important person and a great man. I continued to see George on a fairly regular basis until he died."

Sandy is another political activist on his own. In law school he was president of the Student Bar Association and very active with moot court. And he was on law review. Upon graduation, he became involved in what was then called the Junior Bar Association, and is now called the Young Lawyers, where he was elected president, then a member of the Dade County Bar Association board of directors. He says, "My belief is that bar activities are essential to lawyers who want to stay in touch with what is going on in their profession. Lawyers who are connected to the bar association are lawyers who care about lawyer's ethics issues, and the ideas of professionalism."

Although he eventually became president of the ABA, his first entry into the ABA was slow to come. When asked to be a part of it by his friend, Chesterfield Smith, Sandy told him, "I don't care anything about the ABA. It opposed integration; was against *Brown v. Board of Education*; it helped block ratification of the treaty against genocide. I supported you as ABA president because I like you and I wanted you to achieve that, but I don't have an interest in getting involved." Chesterfield kept calling and getting told no by Sandy. The third time Chesterfield called he told Sandy that he had formed a committee to study the election laws after the 1972 election and all the Watergate problems. He had already sent out a press release with Sandy's name on it and told him, "Certainly you're not going to embarrass me by making me withdraw the press release, because I've already issued it." Sandy says, "That's the way Chesterfield did business."

The rest is history and after serving in many varied capacities in the ABA, he ended up running for president. In the fall of 1989, he found himself sitting in the ABA offices after the news of the fall of the

Berlin Wall and all the other dynamic things were happening in central Europe. He had been Dean of the Florida State University Law School between 1984 and 1989 and he says, "It occurred to me that we needed to fund an ABA initiative that would be a *pro bono* effort by American lawyers to help people in these democracies. That was the birth of the ABA CEELI (Central and Eastern European Law Initiative), which has evolved as a world-wide initiative. The rest is history.

Sandy still has an active practice and fruitful life. He advises lawyers to "lead a life that is productive in terms of public service. Don't get so focused on billable hours that you lose track of the reason you wanted to become a lawyer in the first place. Then for the litigators, I would give them the advice that I got from a crusty old judge when I first became a lawyer. He told me that the only way to be a litigator in a big practice was to determine that you were going to hit the dog closest to you with his mouth widest open." Sandy has the best sense of humor and, of course, that is great advice.

# Your Legacy Is the Number of Lives You Change

*Alan Kopit*

In 1965, Alan Kopit's father owned a "grungy, little store, with a cement floor basement and a linoleum floor upstairs." But to Alan, all that mattered was location—his father's shop was right in the middle of Cleveland's legal district. "Many of his customers were lawyers and they would come through the store on their way to court because you had to pass the store to get there." Alan remembers one specific time when a lawyer stopped in and handed him a long list of Christmas gifts he needed to pick up for judges and other lawyers. "I realized that I had always really liked the law. That was a defining moment in my life when, during the holiday season where everybody was in a great mood and had time to talk, I sat down with the lawyers and really got a sense of what they did for a living. They were well-known in Cleveland. They were community leaders as well as leaders in the legal profession. It was a very inspiring time."

Alan's childhood holiday memory stuck with him as he pursued his law degree, and after graduating he made a conscious decision to head back home to Cleveland. "Cleveland was the third largest corporate headquarters for the Fortune 500 in 1977 when I graduated from law school, so it had all the professionals in both accounting and law firms that go along with that kind of corporate concentration. It was the right choice for me, and I worked at the same law firm for thirty-nine years. I guess I made the right choice."

Around this time, Alan became involved in the White House Fellowships, through a woman named Diane Yu, who is now at New York University. "She interested me in applying for a White House Fellowship, which is a fellowship where you get to work as special assistant with a cabinet secretary. Every year, about one thousand students apply and about ten to twelve are selected. I was fortunate to be selected by the Secretary of Defense, Caspar Weinberger, to be his special assistant."

Alan's fellowship was during the Reagan administration, and as Alan puts it, "I got to see him quite often." Alan took his experience back to Cleveland, where he remained very active in the legal community, as well as the ABA. "I think I used the fellowship correctly and it gave me an experience that is renewed each year when we go back for the White House Fellows reunion every year—it's an annual event."

Alan didn't just stop at the White House though. He was a consumer law contributor for the *Today Show* on NBC for six and a half years, but he says his years in the Young Lawyers Division of the ABA were some of the most important in terms of his personal growth, professional enhancement, and his commitment to public service and, in particular, the public's understanding of the law. "That is carried through later both as chair of the Standing Committee on Public Education, of being on the Presidential Commission on Civic Education, and in my role as Chair of the Fund for Justice and Education, which provides over $60 million of public service money for public service programming on behalf of the American Bar Association. I'm pretty proud of that, but it all started in Young Lawyers Division." He still says his first ABA meeting, at the Plaza Hotel in New York City, was one of the "craziest" experiences of his life.

However, his second event, in Honolulu, really sold him on the idea of participating in the public service work of the ABA. "I had an opportunity to meet Elaine and Allan Tannenbaum. Allan was a lawyer in Atlanta and Elaine was a schoolteacher who had just given birth to a son." The notion of it almost brought tears to his eyes as we talked. "For whatever reason, we struck up a friendship that night, which has truly helped me to understand the importance of family, the importance of your faith, the importance of giving back to the community, and the importance of being a good lawyer and a good father and a good husband." The main thing Allan Tannenbaum taught Alan? "You've got to be a good lawyer, that's a given, but you can add to that if you can give back to your community and to the public."

Alan still believes that giving back is one of his greatest satisfactions in life. "I'm willing to give up time so that the public will better understand the importance of the law in our society." He credits the ABA as being at the top in attempting to open the public's eyes to better understanding the work of lawyers on a daily basis. On a local level, Alan is president of the board of a high-performing charter school that gives struggling inner-city kids the "opportunity to be in a vigorous learning environment without fear of their safety." Alan truly believes in making a difference and giving back, both within and outside of his career as a lawyer. Above all, though, he continues to stress the importance of public service.

"I just hope law students coming out today bear in mind that they do have an obligation to the public. They do play a special role in our society. We're charged with knowing the law; that's a big responsibility in a democracy like ours. With that responsibility comes an obligation and a duty to go out and help the public understand their rights and once they do that, I think they'll find that a lot of the issues with respect to making a living fall into place because you become a better lawyer, you become a better person, and you become very satisfied with the choice you made to become a lawyer."

# Try the Unusual in Your Pursuit of Excellence

*Jeffrey M. Allen*

Jeff was born in Chicago and he lived on the south side, which, at that time, was a Jewish ghetto. When he was about six, he moved to California to a town called Fresno, which is an agricultural community in the central San Joaquin Valley area of the state. Fresno was the Valley's agribusiness center. It was the 1950s and '60s and the evolution of the individual rights was on the forefront. Liberty movements, race relations, and integration in the South were all occurring simultaneously.

The defining moment that shaped Jeff's life was the death of his father when he was eleven years old. He says, "I went to public school my entire life. My father died four days after my eleventh birthday, and my mother went back to school. She had dropped out of school when she married my father. She went back to school and got her college degree and became a teacher." He continues, "When my father died, that was a traumatic experience, but my father knew he was going to die. He had had rheumatic fever as a child, and he got it for the second time when he was in the US Army Air Forces in World War II. It was misdiagnosed, and by the time they figured out what he had, there was permanent damage done to his heart. He died in 1959. My father knew he wasn't going to be around to see my sisters and me grow up."

What his father said to him in the instructions he left before he died has haunted Jeff his whole life and has shaped who he is since he was eleven. Jeff says, "He wrote in a sealed letter, which was kept with his will, that there was not to be a eulogy for him because 'the lives of his children would be his eulogy.'"

That sentence stuck with Jeff because he felt like he was not only responsible for his own life, but "I was responsible for the record of my father's," he says. Jeff describes the profound effect this statement has had on his life, "Everything that I have done in my life, I thought about in those terms. I was the oldest child of three. When I got in high school I was injured and spent a bunch of time in a cast. I couldn't do much in the way of physical activity and took up competitive speaking. I joined the debate team and found out I was exceptionally good at it. As a result of that, I decided maybe I should be a lawyer instead of a doctor. I entered law school in 1970 and got a law degree in 1973."

Like so many lawyers of a certain age, Perry Mason was their role model on television. Jeff remarks, "When I started out in law school, I started out with what I call a 'Perry Mason complex.' But by the time I graduated law school, I had done enough work with criminal law that I never wanted to see it again."

His decision to go to law school was made in high school as the result of the success he had on the debate team and he says, "I never looked back. I always planned from that point forward on being a lawyer. The only two things I ever wanted to be were a doctor or a lawyer. And I switched in high school."

Jeff has used his speaking skills not only as a lawyer, but he also teaches college. He says, "I love teaching. I've taught all my life. If the world was a different place, I might have been a teacher as a career as opposed to a lawyer. I come from a long line of teachers. My grandfather was a teacher; my mother was a teacher; my mother's sister was a teacher; my wife is a teacher; my wife's sister is a teacher; and I've taught my entire adult life as an avocation. I like the idea of taking information that I have and sharing it with a new generation of people who are going to go out and educate another generation. I've taught at the university level for a number of years, but I also taught soccer as a coach, and I taught classes for soccer coaches. I would teach a class of soccer coaches that may have been thirty or forty soccer coaches, and they would each go out and have a team, so I am now influencing three hundred soccer players in a year—from one class."

No matter how much success he has in whatever area he is participating in, he knows that, "What I do is a reflection not only on me but also on my father. If he had just simply said that statement to me and he had lived to be a ripe old age, it would not have had the impact that it did. He had to die to punctuate his statement for me. His death put an exclamation point on it, underscored it, and put it in boldface print in large type. I always tried to do my best because I felt that I should, but it wasn't just for me. It was for me, and it was also because of my father. I won't say there hasn't been a day that I haven't thought about it, but there probably hasn't been a week in my life that I haven't thought about it."

Jeff feels that the statement by his father was not just a moral compass, but that it was a "work ethic compass too." He says, "Maybe I'm giving him more credit than he was due, I don't know. My assumption has always been that he did it intentionally; that he had the foresight to figure out he was not going to be there, and this might be a way that he could be there and influence me. It was at least worth a try. So, he took the shot, and he hit a bull's-eye. Everywhere. It did not make any difference what it was. Whatever it was I was doing, it was how my father would be defined. He chose to define his life by what my sisters and I did. I always tried to maintain a higher standard than standard practice." Jeff's father would be proud of him. Legacy has been a guiding force in his life since that fateful day when he was eleven.

# Make a Positive Difference in the Lives You Serve

*Wm. T. (Bill) Robinson, III*

Bill had an easygoing personality and was a kind and happy man. Once during an American Bar Association (ABA) meeting, I stood near a balcony and saw him enter the room below. He walked with a brisk pace, a big smile on his face, and his eager eyes scanned the room. His countenance was perceivable from that far away. Of course, I tried to hang over the ledge and call out to him. He waved back up at me as if he wanted to jump up and fly to greet me. His enthusiasm was contagious.

Bill was a special person. He came from a devout Catholic family and from very humble beginnings. After our interview, he was dogged in his support of me and my writing career. He read my first legal thriller, *Crosstown Park,* and loved it so much he bought a bunch of them for his friends for Christmas and wrote a great review on Amazon. Even though he was a giant of a man, he was easy to talk to and made everyone feel as if they were talking to an old friend. He was generous with his time and with his enthusiasm for life.

The cornerstone of Bill's life was his faith, and he lived the consummate spiritual life. This doesn't mean he was perfect and always had his ducks in a row. It means that he was a work in progress—always looking for ways to do things faster, better, stronger, and in keeping with godly principles.

Bill was guided in large part by his intuition because he felt, as I do, that the Holy Spirit speaks to you through your intuition. He practiced his faith each day. He says, "I am truly a greater Cincinnatian and that has been my home all my life.

My mom and dad are the heroes of my life. My dad was in the South Pacific fighting in the Second World War when I was born in 1945. My mother was the youngest of nine and was the first to graduate from high school. They were part of the greatest generation, and their focus was on the education of their children. That was their primary goal in life— for their children to get the education they never had the chance to get. When I say we were poor financially, I want to emphasize we were not poor in any other way. It was a very positive childhood."

His work ethic was formed at an early age. He shares, "I started cleaning garbage cans and ashtrays, and doing floors when I was in the third grade and my brother was in the first grade. I felt privileged every day of my life because I saw the way my parents were working for us and we were privileged to work with them, and it was all toward our education. I was an All-City basketball player through the Friars Club, which was a couple of blocks from my small, Catholic elementary school. I went to mass every day. The nuns taught me every grade of elementary school and I can still name every one of them. It was around 1959, and I'll never forget them. They laid my educational foundation for the rest of my life.

People ask me, 'What did they do?' The nuns convinced me to believe in my dreams, to recognize that I could achieve anything I set out to achieve if I worked hard enough and was determined enough, sacrificed enough, and stayed focused on my goal. Coming from my background—success equaled a combination of faith, discipline, and strong educational foundation; in other words, we crossed every 't' and dotted every 'i'."

One thing Bill learned from his parents is "that if you focus on an ultimate goal with passion and determination, the speed bumps in the driveway, the steps we have to take, and the challenges we have to deal with are simply opportunities to move us toward that ultimate goal and should not, in and of themselves, be deterrents. They just must be dealt with, not because they are in the way, but because they are on the avenue to success. My dad used to say, 'When you can do the little things right, you will do the bigger things better.' And I never forgot that." That has always been one of my favorite sayings and it is a little different. Mine is "If you step over the little things, eventually you will step over the big things."

It is not surprising that Bill wanted, like many good Catholic boys, to be a priest. His priest, Father Louis P. Boyle, gave a sermon he never forgot about getting that seminary education. Bill remembers, "He said, 'If you think, if you even suspect, that God might want you to be a priest, do you want to go through your whole life wondering if you should have done it? If you come here, it will be a great education. We'll teach you about life. If you decide that being a priest is not for you, you'll have a good foundation to go out into the world and be success-ful. If you find it is your calling, you'll find a wonderful life of spiritual fulfillment and happiness.' Being a fairly independent kid and having worked virtually every day with my family, for my dad, that made a lot of sense to me and I made up my mind to do it. My mother, of course, immediately identified me as a future pope."

Bill went on to go to college at the seminary and in the summer of 1964, he came home, visited with the parents, and did a little part-time job as a barber. He remembers a defining moment of his life, "I was cut-ting hair the day that John Kennedy was shot. Of course, the seminary shut down. We all went to the chapel to pray for the president. When I went home that summer, my plan was to go back to the seminary. Then, when I was introduced as, 'This is Bill Robinson. He's going to be a priest,' I realized it just didn't fit. Something did not ring right when I heard myself introduced that way. For the previous five years, that's all I wanted to be was a priest. That is what I saw myself being. And then in less than thirty days, I changed my mind. I think it was divine providence."

Armed with this new revelation Bill drove up to the seminary to see Father Boyle, the spiritual director. "His initial remarks had really per-suaded me to go to the seminary. I explained to him what was happen-ing. He said, 'Let me explain something to you. The last time I checked, nobody around here is getting an apparition, an appearance from God or the Blessed Mother. It just doesn't happen that way. *God speaks to us through our intuition.* That's the way God speaks to us. It sounds to me like God is speaking to you. We should always listen when we think God is communicating with us. It sounds to me like you need to get out there in the world and see what your destiny is. If you find out you want to come back, we'd love to have you. It's been great to have you here, but you need to explore this. You need to find out what this is about.'"

But now he had to tell his family. Bill said, "I waited for the right moment at Sunday dinner when there was a lull in the action. I said, 'Hey, everybody. I've got something to tell you.' People started dropping things on and off. Did I rob a bank? What happened here? It sounded dramatic and it was. I said, 'I'm not going back to the seminary.' My mother looks across the table and said, 'What are you going to do with your life?' As if there was really nothing else I could do. And I understood that. I said, 'Well, Mom, I've thought about it, I've prayed about it. I've decided I'm going to try to be a lawyer.'"

Bill realized that he saw life as a calling. He says, "Vocation is a big word in the Catholic Church—it's a calling to serve, a calling to make a positive difference in the lives of others. It's our purpose for being here. Intuition is what told me to be a lawyer. I was a devotee of Thomas Moore. I read *To Kill a Mockingbird*. I read about lawyers. Back then, everything I read about lawyers was positive and about service, about making a positive difference in people's lives. It seemed to me that it would be the career I most logically connected with and would be the most fulfilling. These were the primary reasons I had gone to the seminary—to try to make a positive difference in the lives of other people. My mother sat back and looked at me and without missing a beat, she said, 'My God. From a saint to a sinner.' Then she laughed. She was a great mom, of course. She came over and gave me a big hug."

When he made that decision not only did he not know a lawyer, he had never met a lawyer. But he just knew. He says, "It seemed logical to me that this was the way, and I still truly believe that a career in the law, even in today's tough economic times, is still the most meaningful avenue for professional service that a person can choose. By choosing law, one is assured of an endlessly fascinating, complex, interesting, challenging, fatiguing, fulfilling experience in life. And because it is all those things and more, success, real success, in the law can only be achieved with passion. It requires passion to generate the energy that is needed to do so much where there is so little time when resources are not enough. I don't have the words or the adjectives to capture fully how wonderful a career in the law is. That applies to everyone, virtually everyone I know, in the law. Does that mean everyone is equally successful? No. Does it mean that everyone's practice is like everyone else's practice? No. But that is the fascination of it."

Bill is not reticent about the bumps in the road along the way to success. Everyone has them. He says in his humorous style, "I'm a guy who could not get elected student bar president, student government president, local county bar president, and I end up president of the American Bar Association. I want young people to understand that is life. How you handle your defeats tells people more about you as a person than how you handle your victories. Most people are good winners, but not everybody is a good loser. People are going to lose, and you find out what people are all about when they lose. When someone says, 'Lawyer so-and-so never lost a case,' my response is that he or she hasn't tried many cases. We learn more from our defeats than we ever learn from our victories. That is a fact of life."

Bill gave me his LEAD line with no hesitation, "Make a positive difference in the lives you serve. That is my LEAD line because that is the purpose for being a lawyer. It is not the money, not the cars, not the houses, and not the second houses. It is your service to others that counts." He was passionate about reading obituaries. He said, "When I talk to younger people, I ask, 'Who reads obituaries?' They all look around. Of course, they don't read obituaries! I tell them to look at them and to call me if they ever read one that says, 'So-and-so died and owned three Mercedes and two houses, or this amount of jewelry.' No. Scientists tell us that millions of years after evolutionary development and mostly progress in the human race, what is identified as worth mentioning in every human being's life at the end is—family, worship, community, and then maybe innovative business success. None of us should ever be measured by the quality of our car or the size of our home, and if that is your goal, you are doomed to a life of frustration."

Bill makes us all think about how we view our profession and our passion for our purpose. Are we living and walking in our vocation? Bill's inspiring legacy will live on for many years beyond his life. It was an honor to be his friend.

# PART 2
# Excellence

# Be Ethical, Return Calls, Keep a Clean Desk

*Dennis W. Archer*

Dennis gives sound, practical advice for his LEAD line and it forms the basis of the leadership principle of excellence. He says, "'Always be ethical' is practical because you can lose your law license in the same amount of time that it will take you to start law school, take your first exam, and get your grades back if you violate the Canons of Ethics. Nothing is worth that. 'Returning your phone calls timely' is important because even the nagging client may give you a referral or refer you your biggest case one day. 'Keep a clean desk' sends the right message when you go out to the lobby and bring your clients back into your office; they see it and think the only thing you have got to do in life is take on their work."

Dennis was born in Detroit, Michigan, in 1942. Joe Lewis, the heavyweight champion boxer, lived right across from him. Dennis says, "He was a source of pride in our neighborhood, and I grew up with that pride of him inside me." When he was five, his family moved to Cassopolis, Michigan, and for the first few years they did not have running water or a bathtub in the house. He says, "That meant Saturday night was metal tub bath night."

Dennis has come a long way in life from those humble beginnings, but he never forgets where he came from. He says, "My life experiences have taught me what it is like to need, how to reach for the stars while still respecting people and holding them in the highest regard." His parents "instilled the value that if you want something, you've got to work for it, you've got to save your money to buy it, and something that is worth having is worth working for or saving for."

His father had a third-grade education and his mother had a high school diploma. Just before he was born, his father lost his arm just above his left elbow. He was a veteran of the US Army and he worked for a man who owned a tool and die shop in South Bend, Indiana, and a summer home on Diamond Lake. Dennis recalls, "My dad made $75 every two weeks for six months of the year and $37.50 the other six months of the year. There were times especially during the time when he was getting $37.50 every two weeks, every now and then, my dad would have to go down to the Department of Social Services, to get a check to help ends meet. There were times when I was always full, but there were dinners of biscuits with no honey or jam. We drank sassafras tea made from roots. Dad was a good hunter and he would hunt during the winter for rabbits and squirrels. He was an excellent cook. He taught me how to work with electricity and taught me how to tend a garden."

Dennis remembers, "My first job was at eight when I served as a caddy on the golf course. My next job was to set pins in a bowling alley." Early on, he saw the importance of hard work. "Hard work produces excellence in one's character." In high school he worked at a bakery. He says, "I walked a mile in the early morning to go in and sweep and mop the floor. I would go back home, sleep half an hour, and then go to school. Edwin Johnson owned a metal business. He must have seen me walking by in the early mornings and must have liked my tenacity, my willingness to work, and my work ethic because he asked me to stop going downtown and to come work for him after school. I soldered and welded and did a lot of wire brushing to clean off the welding or soldering spots."

Dennis worked in a drugstore and was impressed by the pharmacist. He went to register at Wayne State University upon his high school graduation and when they asked what he wanted to be, he said a pharmacist. He says, "I didn't have a clue. It took me nearly two years before pharmacy and I did not agree with each other. I transferred to Western Michigan University in Kalamazoo where I met an outstanding counselor and he gave me some great advice. He asked what I wanted to do. I said, 'I'd like to teach high school history' and I was told that there was a glut of teachers in that area. My roommate was majoring in special education for the educable mentally retarded, so I thought that would be good for me. I graduated from Western Michigan University, came back to the North, started teaching in Detroit public schools and became a tenured teacher. I loved it."

But Dennis wanted to keep going with his career. To be a principal you had to get a master's degree, so he started off at the off-campus site of the University of Michigan. He saw that he had the same textbooks in the master's program that he had in undergrad and the teacher he was dating at the time said, "Why don't you go to law school?" Dennis says he had no idea at the time what lawyers did. He says, "The more she talked about it, the more I wanted it, the more she talked about it . . . I finally took the LSAT exam and the exam score suggested that if I were to enroll in law school, chances are if I applied myself, I would be able to graduate. There was no guarantee that if you go to law school you're going to graduate. There is no guarantee that if you go to law school and you graduate, that you're going to pass the bar. There's no law school that I know of that promises you that if you go to law school, you graduate, you pass the bar, that you're going to go into the practice area that you like. Or that you're going to be wealthy or whatever you might have in mind for the future. With that as a backdrop, I started law school and along the way did the smartest thing I've ever done and that was I married my fellow teacher, Trudy, and the woman who encouraged me to go to law school."

Dennis started law school in 1966 and his first job was as a gofer at an African American law firm in the city of Detroit in 1967. He says, "During the summer of 1967 Detroit experienced a riot. The police rounded up several thousand people and put them in jail and the call came out to all lawyers in the metropolitan area to come in and represent them. I watched these outstanding lawyers represent people who were charged with offenses and most of the charges were dismissed. I saw the majesty of what a lawyer could do on behalf of someone who was in trouble, who could not afford a lawyer, who couldn't get a lawyer during an emergency. That was really a beautiful eye-opener for me."

The next summer he had the opportunity to be a summer associate at Ford Motor Company in the Office of the General Counsel. He then applied at a large Detroit law firm and before he went in for the interview, he researched the person he was meeting with on Martindale-Hubbell. The lawyer politely told him that their law firm did not hire anybody who graduated from the Detroit College of Law and that they only hire people from the University of Michigan and from places like Harvard. Dennis remembers, "I thought to myself, 'Well, isn't this something?' Because the Martindale-Hubbell profile of this lawyer said he graduated from the Detroit College of Law."

Dennis felt it was, from the lawyer's point of view, a polite way of turning him down because "at that time there were no lawyers of color who were an associate or a partner in any large law firm in the city of Detroit." Dennis says, "After I graduated from law school, I joined a small African American law firm. I won my very first case that I tried. It was a criminal case and the judge I tried it before ultimately became a member of the Michigan Supreme Court and I took his spot when he was elevated from the Michigan Supreme Court to the Sixth Circuit Court of Appeals. I never served as a judge before. I went straight from trial practice to become a judge on the Michigan Supreme Court."

Once of Dennis' exciting lawyer experiences was when he got to be Rosa Park's guardian ad litem in a case against a record company and a group that sang a song that she did not like the words to that were "inconsistent with who she was." Johnnie Cochran was representing her, and he died a couple of months before Dennis began his representation. The case was eventually settled.

Before his term as the first African American ABA president, Dennis got to serve as the president of the National Bar Association that was formed because there was a time when "lawyers of color, and in particular, African Americans, could not join the ABA." He says, "There is nothing like being a lawyer." He came out of the "old school" tradition with people like George Bushnell from Michigan, who was a former president of the ABA, and others deeply involved in the civil rights movement like Federal Judge Damon Keith and Judge George W. Crockett, Jr., who was a judge in Detroit and a US congressman.

He says, "The practice of law is a calling and sometimes that calling is to public service. I had had the privilege of serving on the Michigan Supreme Court and then later becoming mayor of the city of Detroit and I was trying to make a difference in the lives of our citizens here in the city. Then I was president of the National League of Cities representing some 18,000 cities, villages, and towns around the United States on issues that are important to our residents."

Excellence has to do with ethics for Dennis. He says, "There is nothing that beats hard work preparation and respect for everybody. Respect for the judges; never misleading judges; never misleading juries; never misleading clients; just basic ethics. Ethics became part of me when I first started practicing law and Governor William Milliken appointed me to the State Board of Ethics. Shortly thereafter, I became a member of the House of Delegates of the American Bar Association and we had our first big ethics issue in terms of the Kutak Commission. The application of the ABA model rules was always a topic and it helped me on the Michigan Supreme Court. All lawyers have an obligation to be mindful of and respect our professional code of conduct. As a jurist there are judicial canons of ethics, which cause you to avoid even the appearance of impropriety."

When he thinks about the leadership qualities he has derived in his rich and colorful life he says, "I recognize what I don't know. You learn that as a lawyer. I learned listening skills from being on the Michigan Supreme Court. I learned fighting and being an advocate for my city by being a trial lawyer and representing clients. I understood the value of being a teacher by working with my constituents when I was mayor. I had open books and I didn't hide anything because I wanted the opposition to appreciate that a lawyer of color could lead with distinction and hopefully make everybody proud of what I was doing."

When Dennis walked down the aisle to accept the nomination to become president-elect of the American Bar Association, he had Sissy Marshall, Thurgood Marshall's widow, on one arm and US Senator Hillary Rodham Clinton on the other. In 2016 he was awarded the ABA Medal, the ABA's highest honor at the ABA Annual Meeting in San Francisco. He continues to receive awards and to do good work.

Throughout all of his successes and accomplishments I cannot stop picturing Dennis as a young boy working happily doing jobs like setting the bowling pins or sweeping the floor. I can't help but think he was viewed by his elders as a young man with great character and promise. He says, "They probably saw more in me than I saw in myself." I asked him if his wife Trudy was still his inspiration and with his warm humor he said, "She reminds me of that every day!" Dennis Archer's life embodies excellence, and I suggest we all follow his LEAD line for success.

# Out of the Hottest Furnace Comes the Hardest Steel

*Jim Perdue, Sr.*

"My father was an alcoholic and an abuser. My mother was a saint."

Jim Perdue, Sr. started off our conversation telling me a story about a time in high school when his father was physically abusing his mother. "I had gotten big enough to do something about it. I took him on and ran him off. He never lived with us again. The teachers at the high school all knew what I had gone through, and I was named outstanding senior by the faculty. Having to confront your father left an impression on me. But I will tell you that you would never find a more hopeless, almost semi-tragic figure, than I was in the summer of 1957."

That summer, Jim graduated high school and was looking for a job. He remembers, "I graduated at the top of my class in high school and always had good grades. I studied hard. It wasn't because I was smart; I just worked hard. But I enjoyed school." He knew he wanted to go to college, and he knew he wanted to go to law school. But he didn't know how to get there. "God works miracles through people. There are those who believe you can't have a miracle unless you have something supernatural. I've never believed that. I've always felt that God works his miracles through his children."

Jim's first miracle came through Bill Kilgarlin, who offered Jim a debate scholarship at the University of Houston. His second miracle came through Elro and Statie Mae

Brown, the parents of Jim's high school best friends. They pointed him toward a job, handling the night shift at a smelter. He worked for two months until he saved up enough to put down a payment on a car. "I had a car and I had a job, which got me into my first semester. I would go to work at the smelter at 4:00, get off at midnight, go home and study, and make the next morning class. I was able to get through that way."

That was, until the recession hit in 1962 and Jim lost his job at the smelter. But again, another miracle came through for him. He went to see Senior Federal Judge Woodrow Seals, who was then a US Attorney, and told him "Mr. Seals, I am broke, and I've got one semester left to graduate. I don't have any money and I don't have a job." Woodrow picked up the telephone and called Jack Proctor, who was at that time the managing partner of Fulbright and Jaworski. Woodrow could con anybody into anything, I mean, he had great political skills. He told Jack, 'Jack, do you guys ever hire summer clerks?' At the time, they didn't. But they made an exception for me."

Finally, Jim was on the path he had been dreaming of since the sixth grade, when he first got it in his mind to be a lawyer. Back then, his social studies teacher had the class do a debate on whether Texas should divide into five separate states, as the state constitution allows. "I remember enjoying that debate so much, and of course, my mother being a legal secretary, I would go down and see her at work in her office. My dad would come in when he had work, and he always had on a T-shirt with grease on it and Camel cigarettes rolled up in the sleeve."

"I told myself that I didn't want to be like that. I'm one of those people who wanted to be everything my dad was not." Jim told me about his father's habit of writing hot checks and sending Jim into the store to pick them up because his father "couldn't face them." "I guess I had this burning need to be accepted and recognized and respected. It just came out very early that I had that drive."

One of his most trying times in his life was when he was trying a case while the woman he was engaged to was dying of cancer. He says, "That was the hardest case I ever tried. It was a good case; we got a good result. But it's very hard to try a case when the woman you love is in the hospital dying. And she died, I think the day we argued the case or maybe the day after. Her funeral was the day the jury came in with the verdict. I remember that."

Jim got into medical malpractice early on in his career and his first book was *The Law of Texas Medical Malpractice,* published by the University of Houston Press. He then wrote a book with Jim Sales on product liability. Then he did a book called *Who Will Speak for the Victim?* that has sold many copies all over the country.

Jim told me about a moment that stood out in his legal career. He was at a meeting of the Inner Circle, the top 100 trial lawyers in the country. They were discussing the downfalls of losing a case versus the highs of winning a case. "There are ups and downs in the practice of law. When you lose a case, you come home, and you go to bed, and you might not get out of bed for two or three days. You win a case, you come home, and you can't wait to get to the office the next morning because you want to talk to everybody. People are calling you about the great victory you had. The first big verdict I got was in 1968 and Mike Gann and I tried the case where a fellow was operating a gantry crane, a crane that's real tall and it's up on railroad tracks with wheels. That was my first big victory and everybody in town was talking about it. It was like $280,000 and people thought, my gosh, how do you get that kind of money? But this was in 1968 and there were no million-dollar verdicts. Then I got my first million-dollar verdict in the 1970s on a brain-damaged child case. A little girl was injured during a routine cosmetic surgery."

"My defining moments were back when it looked so hopeless. Any time I get down, all I have to go back and think about the way it was when I was young. I just remember how I felt, and it was like the world was coming to an end. Somehow, through the help of all these wonderful people, I got out of that kind of life. That's why if I find somebody I can help, I'm always going to help them. Because I had so many people help me. If somebody had come and told me that summer of 1957 that I would end up where I am today, I would say they were delusional."

Jim is still very active today. When Jim isn't litigating, he teaches a courtroom storytelling class at University of Houston Law Center. He remembers trying a case in Jasper, Texas, when a court reporter came up to him and said "Perdue, you think the old saying is true that every trial lawyer just has so many bullets in his gun? He wakes up one day and realizes it's empty?" Jim replied, "Oh, not me. I'm going to try them until they pull me down."

Jim Perdue, Sr. is a legendary trial lawyer that came from humble beginnings and now devotes his life to teaching law students how to tell stories and to become amazing trial lawyers. I would say it is a great full circle.

# Fill Up the Boat Before You Take Off

*R. William "Bill" Ide, III*

"My early years shaped things about me that I did not understand until later."

Bill grew up with a loving mother and an alcoholic father. "In the calm, he was wonderful, but in the storm, he was very much a bully." It took Bill a while to truly find himself and he is still searching to this day. "I understand now that I want to live in the moment of today. I don't want regrets of yesterday or the fears of tomorrow. I want to understand why I react in certain ways."

During the storm of Bill's childhood, school provided a refuge. He recalls one teacher in particular who saw his need for positive reinforcement and fulfilled it. "It sounds very small now, but at the time, it was very important." Bill learned how to be a bully from his father, and how to fight from his grandfather, and he thought being tough and mean was the best way to gain recognition. Unfortunately, his small stature made it hard for him to be intimidating. "I have this theory that when you have those hard times, and you are a male, or if sports are hard for you, or you are a slow learner—the ones that are farther along physically have not learned disappointment and the frustration yet, getting knocked down and getting back up. And you have to learn that." Bill grew up being afraid to try, and it reflected in his grades. Fortunately, the headmaster at his school saw through that, and recommended Bill to Washington and Lee University, where he was accepted.

When Bill started college, he was still anxious about trying to reach his full potential, and his grades continued to slip. He joined a fraternity, which interestingly became a turning point for his education. "My fraternity made me go to study hall and I was pouting, and I thought since I was there, I might as well read the book. I did, and I made an A. I learned that if I read the books, maybe I could do better." He started applying himself, and then he started seeing results. Eventually, Bill was awarded a scholarship, enabling him to continue attending the university.

By the time he entered law school, Bill was hooked on learning. "I loved history and I was learning about people, constitutional law, and contract law, and it was just all eye-opening to me. My peers were so interesting, and Virginia had a wonderful culture in that we tried really hard. We competed at one level, but there was a civility to it. It was wonderful." At the end of his first semester, Bill found himself in the top 10 percent of his class. His friend turned to him and said, "I didn't know you were smart." There was great shock on his face. Bill wanted to say, "You're right, I didn't either."

When it was time to get a job, Bill wrote a letter to Judge Griffin Bell at the Fifth Circuit in Atlanta. "Fate would have it that I interviewed, and he gave me a job, so that was a real change for me. The Fifth Circuit was unbelievable. It was literally reweaving the fabric of the South, integrating police departments, integrating school, and so for a year, we were in the middle of it. It was so exciting. It was action all the time." While Bill was there, he flew under the wing of Judge Bell, who became something of a mentor and a hero to Bill. "Judge Griffin Bell was one of the more talented individuals. He had a terrific personality. He was very gregarious, and very much a people person. He had a very deep, southern drawl—what we call a south Georgia drawl. He had a terrific sense of humor. Even though he was the judge, he was really more of an executive kind of person. Some judges become monastic, but not Judge Bell."

While Bill was working for the Fifth Circuit, the makeup of the court caused some unrest in the community. There were four very liberal judges who were receiving death threats. Bill witnessed Judge Bell use his resourcefulness and positivity to push through and keep the court in working order, despite all the drama. "That helped me a lot because he was so positive, he believed you should just keep working at it and keep being innovative, and that you will find a solution. I believe that is true."

After leaving the Fifth Circuit, Bill started practicing at King & Spalding, where he worked with Charlie Kirbo, known for being Jimmy Carter's lawyer. He was also a good friend of Judge Bell. "I had a very hard case where all the law was stacked against me. He asked if I had all the facts, and I said, 'Yes, I think I do.' He said, 'You always go by the facts and the equities, and the law will follow you.' That's just what I learned from Judge Bell and Charlie Kirbo."

This was about the time when Bill started getting involved with the ABA Young Lawyers Division. He started meeting people in legal services for the poor, a new idea at the time. "It was all new to me, a new world, new exposure." Bill got the social work gene from his mother, who he described as an "amateur social worker." He saw a need in the community and wanted to be involved. "I got involved with that, and we formed the first, probably in the country, state-wide legal aid program. That was one of the best things I ever did in my life."

I asked him where his confidence came from, how he knew he would succeed in that sort of venture. He credits a lot of his spirit to the culture of Atlanta. "There was such a spirit around here back then of how it could be a better world, and 'We Shall Overcome,' and all those different things. I was mesmerized by it—the idealism, the joy. The black culture is just spectacular with the way they take adversity, and they don't let it get them down. I suppose I was the establishment because I was with one of the blue-chip law firms and they probably embraced me a little bit. That gave them that side of the fence. I got very much involved and started going public defender. The more I was exposed, the more I thought that being able to change people's lives is something that is really important."

In 1971, Bill attended his first ABA meeting. "I didn't know what it was, but it looked interesting. I didn't know anybody, and I was just amazed. Ted Kennedy was speaking, the Chief Justice was speaking, and I went into a room and saw these people. It was very magical." Bill quickly began moving up the ranks. He started getting the Young Lawyers involved in legal services, which quickly became "a big deal." At the mid-year meeting, Bill announced he was running for secretary.

"The Lord just told me to do it. It was sort of crazy. Something happened inside me that told me to run." Bill is a big believer in intuition. Shortly after his successful run for secretary, he received an offer from a small firm, "and something told me I should do it." It ended up being a great move for Bill, even though certain people in his life saw the move as a downsize.

I was curious whether he always went with the underdog, or if he identified with them. He said, "Yes. Because I feel like the vested interests too often pulls up the ladder with no one else in the boat. It lightened the interests that have wealth and power to open up and share. Too often that doesn't happen."

Bill's career kept moving and growing, and so did his involvement with the ABA. He decided to run for president, won, had a great year, and then went back to practicing. "Then all of a sudden, I learned that I had prostate cancer, so that just took over my world for about three months in 1996. I was sure I was going to die, and I was scared to death." Fortunately, he recovered.

Currently, Bill is working on finding a way that corporations can be improved upon. "I think the efficiencies of the private market system are credible for economic prosperity, but the need for high morality and a strong moral compass, and a culture that can be trusted to do that, is more referable than government trying to regulate. They should regulate to a certain degree. I am very much in some corporate circles, and I enjoy in my practice being called in by boards of directors when they have a crisis. You have the white hats and the black hats. You see where you can be helpful."

Wherever life takes him, Bill's driving force is the greater good of the community. "No matter what you do in life, you should always have a motivation for the greater good, and you will do well. Self-interest for our own ego does not work." He credits much of his success from just joining the ABA and working hard.

Bill left me with a story that sums up his work ethic perfectly: "I'll never forget I was in China about two years ago in the middle of nowhere on this highway, and here was this woman, obviously working for the state with a broom, sweeping the highway. Very industrious in that thought. For her, she cared about what she was doing, and she was doing it as well as she could."

# Find Your Unique Abilities and Build Your Life on Them

*Robert Armstrong*

When I sat down with Robert, I was surprised to hear how similar our early childhoods were. Robert and I both felt more at home in educational settings than with our own families, and I found it comforting that most of his defining moments, like many of my own, took place at school.

Growing up in post-World War II Canada, Robert felt that his parents, both products of the Great Depression in Canada, weren't really interested in him. However, as soon as he started school, he "got it in my head that to be a smart little kid is how you can get recognition in the world. My identity started to focus on school because that was where I was getting my recognition, not at home." One of his earliest memories is the love and excitement he felt at the prospect of going to school and the reward of excelling in his studies. Maybe an unusual sentiment for a child of that age, but Robert stuck with it despite receiving few positive affirmations at home.

As Robert continued to show his parents his success, he continued to feel an overall lack of interest on their part. "I made the decision that if they were not going to care about me, I was not going to share anything about my life with them." Although Robert had chosen to make monumental decisions for his own benefit, and keep his parents out of them, his parents continued to make decisions for the family unit when his father decided to move them from Canada to California like something reminiscent of *The Grapes of Wrath*.

"We arrived in California, and that was another defining moment for me. I kicked and screamed and did not want to leave my friends. I wanted to stay in Canada," he says. His father, done with the lack of job prospects in Toronto, piled Robert, his mother, and his two young sisters, Jane and Kathy, into the car and started driving. His mother, seven months pregnant, reached her limit in New Mexico, and flew to California ahead of the rest of the family.

Robert was fifteen and started high school in San Diego. At school, he was again noticed—but this time for something different. "Another defining moment was when I made the decision to lose my Canadian accent. I did it in about two or three weeks. There is no motivation stronger for a young boy with testosterone going through his system than to want to fit in."

He continues, "It was a very scary time emotionally to come to a place where I knew no one, to start in a new school in a new country, and I had to find my way." He found himself gravitating toward the speech and drama department, a place where he had found friends in Canada. This was one of the first times he found himself with a meaningful connection to what he calls his "unique abilities." This theme, discovering unique abilities and staying in touch with them, became a major piece of his professional career. Robert's unique ability was, of course, communication. "I needed to be communicating. I needed to be able to generate the passion and inspiration and speak to people about it."

But even tuning in to your unique abilities doesn't guarantee success. Robert's high school commencement address was not given by the valedictorian, as most traditional high schools operate. Instead, a speaker was chosen by a selection committee. Robert, who had won contests two years in a row already, auditioned. His chosen piece, *The Chambered Nautilus* by Oliver Wendell Holmes, is one that many of us, as lawyers, are well familiar with. ". . . build thee more stately mansions; O my soul, As the swift season roll . . ."

Robert recalls, "We were in a small room and Tim, my competitor, did his speech in a really loud voice, and I gave my speech in a voice, which I thought was appropriate for the size of the room. The teacher who was making the decision said, 'Both of you just did excellent jobs. But, since we're going to be outside in an outdoor arena, I'm going to pick Tim because his voice seems to carry better.'" To Robert, this was a moment where the world was unfair, where the world didn't seem to care about his priorities, his reasons, or his future. But he was able to take it in stride. "I had to get used to that. So, here my opportunity to give the commencement address teetered on my ability to not yell in a small room."

After high school he traveled around the United States and Europe and while in London he worked at the headquarters for the British legal system, the Middle Temple. As a janitor it was his job to sweep the tomb of Oliver Goldsmith. He says, "This was not a glamorous job. On the one corner was the Ploughshare House where Shakespeare presented *The Twelfth Night* for the first time. There was a table that was made out of the bow of the Golden Hind, the ship that Sir Francis Drake sailed around the world. There was the Charles Lamb Building, the Temple, the Goldsmith Building, everything was centered there. All this history; all this tradition. I was just reveling in it.

Meanwhile, my student deferment for Vietnam had run out and I made the craziest decision you can possibly imagine. Here I am. I am a Canadian living in London, and I decide to join the US Navy. I got to the US Embassy in London in Grosvenor Square and I was sworn in and they flew me from London to McGuire Air Force Base in New Jersey and then they took me all the way to Great Lakes, Illinois, and I went through boot camp in the Navy. I got a real taste of what a change of atmosphere was all about.

Then they gave some tests and they found out that I had a little bit of intelligence, so they sent me to school in Newport, Rhode Island. In 1966 I volunteered to go to Vietnam, and they sent me to Danang. I became the admiral's driver and bodyguard. Here I was driving a car, a chase Jeep loaded with weapons behind me. For nineteen months, I drove the admiral and the senators and congressmen who would visit."

Upon his return, he got out of the Navy and went to college and graduated law school in 1976. Robert was not keen on the experience. He says, "I did not like it at all. It just didn't inspire me. I was always afraid that no one would hire me. Rather than trying to get hired, I didn't even apply." After starting a partnership with a friend from law school, like many young lawyers, Robert took the work he could get. "I hated it. I'm not very good at conflict." He and his partner went their own ways, and Robert got hooked on the idea of reinventing himself. "I wanted to do what I wanted to do, and I love public speaking."

However, he wasn't looking for the type of argumentative public speaking that comes with being a litigator. At the same time, he wasn't looking to give up lawyering completely.

Robert entered a graduate program at University of San Diego, did some research, and discovered a little document that few of his contemporaries were using—a revocable inter vivos trust, commonly known as a living trust. "That was the big 'aha' moment for me. I found out that this thing was something that I wanted to investigate and the more I looked at it, the more I thought it was the greatest thing in the world. People needed to know about this." Other estate planning attorneys didn't see the value in it, but Robert didn't give up. In the late 1970s, Robert started advertising free public seminars. "So here I was, this sole practitioner, using my unique abilities. Nobody was doing this, and I had crowds of 50, 60, and 70. I spoke to over 400 people in a room about estate planning, and I would take them through an entire story about somebody who does not plan properly. Then I would have people sign up for appointments, for initial consults, and I started to have clients." The new system Robert created took off and pretty soon he found amazing success.

"It was an absolute marketing juggernaut and was the beginning of a law firm focusing solely on estate planning." Robert took his unique abilities, speaking and communication, and found a way to use them—he built a law firm from the ground up, implemented hundreds of systems to streamline estate planning in a way that was incredibly beneficial to the client, he expanded across the country, and he succeeded.

He started offering the Robert Armstrong Marketing Boot Camp, which was so successful that after the first round, he immediately doubled the price of attendance—and still filled the seats up. In the early 1990s he and his partner created the American Academy of Estate Planning Attorneys. Robert's success continues to endure. He and his partner decided to form a special group inside of the American Academy called the Peak Performer Program. He is able to pour all of his passion and interests into helping people change their mindsets about life and abundance and to show them ways they could reframe their practice and reframe their lives.

Looking back on the healing of his childhood wounds, Robert recalls that much later in life he discovered that he had been reading his parents all wrong. "They came from a time when you didn't have an over-showing of affection as we do now, but they used to tell all of their friends that Robert is doing this, and Robert is doing that." He remembers the training where he realized this. "Tears rolling down my face, I realized I had been punishing my mom and dad for something they never did. The feeling of how unfair I had been washed over me." He set about to set things right with both of them.

"When my dad was eighty years old, I threw a surprise birthday party for him and all of the relatives from Canada came to San Diego. I got to complete things with my dad before he died in 2001." Robert's mother is still alive, and he honored her at the Academy's twentieth anniversary. "We got a chance to stand up in front of the entire membership of the organization, hundreds of people, and pay tribute to our mothers and what contribution they made. We gave them roses and they were like belles of the ball."

He says, "The defining moment for me, as I look back on it now, was that there is no success in life until you are working in the areas of your passion. True success won't come until you have discarded all those things that you're incompetent in or maybe just competent in, and you focus your energy on those things that you were meant to do. That quest about finding what you truly are gifted at should be the task of every young lawyer, every one, and having the courage to say, 'I'm going to find a way to build my practice based upon the gifts that I have, my unique abilities, and I'm going to delegate the rest of the tasks in the law firm to a staff that is built up with them working in their unique abilities.'"

"Where I like to do one thing, somebody else likes to do another, and you build a team or a community around you with a client-centered focus, everyone working in their unique abilities. Now there is not the stress, the anxiety, the dread of a normal law practice. And every lawyer that comes to us saying they are dying, they are burned out, they are looking for something different."

"That's what I've done up to this point. That's what I've done with my life, and I am more fulfilled now from this circuitous journey that brought me here. Now I am truly doing the things that most fulfill me, which is teaching and inspiring and mentoring other lawyers."

# Get Outside Your Comfort Zone

*Alan O. Olson*

Alan was raised in Mankato, Minnesota, in what he calls "a very economically challenged part of town." His early lessons in teamwork were instilled in him whenever it rained. He says, "Whoever was in the house would make a mad dash for the cupboard to get all of the pots and pans to catch as many of the leaks flowing through the roof as possible." But the close-knit family and neighborhood full of "hard-working, open, and honest people who were wired to just feel comfortable in their own skin" gave Alan a great base to draw on.

Alan's neighborhood was very close to a milling plant and there was a very strong aroma that was unpleasant. He felt like they all shared the "same label as being something other than on an equal playing field with the folks who did not live on the prairie or on the other side of the tracks." He appreciates the fact that he got a chance to grow up around people who were "well-grounded, very patriotic folks, who worked hard and wore things like love and praise on their sleeves. It was a place where you didn't grow up with airs. Everybody was very open and candid and honest about their viewpoints and how they felt. There was a very high emphasis on being respectful, being interested in other people's daily goings-on and their families' accomplishments."

Alan points out that despite being on the lower rungs of society at that time, the people were wonderful and that appreciation of people from different walks of life has been something that has guided him throughout his life. He says, "It was a very outgoing bunch of people, but very simple. I mean, many of the folks had limited education. My mother had a high school degree, and my father went as far as the tenth grade. Like so many of the people who were our neighbors, they were two of the most intelligent people I've ever met in my life. I was very proud to be their son."

Alan is very clear about his purpose in life and he states unequivocally, "Without question, the over-arching guiding force of my life for as far back as I can remember, and to this day, has always been dedicated to pouring everything that I have in terms of energy, strategy, intelligence, friends, and networks into leveling the playing field for the have-nots because that's what I had: an up-close and personal look at growing up. I was very sensitive to how misunderstood very good people could be simply because they lacked money and status. For that reason, they were labeled as being something inferior, and in fact, quite the contrary was the case. If you were looking for thoroughly decent, good people, this was where you found them. Those are the folks that I had the good fortune of being influenced by growing up."

Alan felt the discrimination of being looked at funny when people found out where he was from. He was fortunate to do well in school, so he didn't fit the normal mold of people coming from the prairie or the other side of the tracks. He remarked that early on most people didn't really know where you're from—he was just another kid in class. He says, "One of the things that I think distinguished me, and this was directly from the influence of where I grew up, is I was always seen as being mature for my age in terms of being polite and dedicated to being respectful of other people. Politeness was a very big thing in my household and neighborhood. It was very important to me to take the time to get to know people and to understand their viewpoints. I think those were probably the earlier roots of my fascination with my college major, sociology. My first love has always been understanding individual behavior in a group context."

Around his senior year in high school Alan began to think that he might become a lawyer because if he wanted to dedicate his life to leveling the playing field for the have-nots, the best post to do it from was the legal system. He says, "A big part of my identity was championing the causes of others, but particularly those who were picked on, and were labeled, and were ostracized. For example, I remember a time on the playground around third grade where there was a boy who was being more than just picked on verbally and physically. He was actually being beaten up by three different boys at once. Although I never had any delusions of being able to win such a fight, I found myself compelled to go in and help this boy for as long as I could because I could not stand by idly on the sidelines. While I did not know anything really about fighting per se, I did have some wrestling moves I utilized to try to help him. They were surprised that someone would dare stand up to the 'in' popular boys. I had to get in there and try to do everything I could to help him. I think that experience had a profound effect on my life's compass."

The fight was eventually broken up by the playground attendant. Alan realized that things were not as black and white as he once thought. He says, "What you learn about it is it isn't so much about whether you 'won or lost' as it was about whether you tried your best to make a meaningful and lasting difference in the lives of real people about things that you felt passionate and strongly about. Did you leave things better than when you came? Did you take the blessings that you were given and put them to work to try to make things better?"

"Throughout my life, and to this day, this is what I do on a daily basis. I'm a plaintiff's lawyer so I represent the have-nots against the most powerful and well-funded of systems that exist. I try to do it in a very respectful manner for those that I go up against, but at the same time, that's how I have an abiding conviction to serve."

Alan was viewed as a leader from an early age because he is a good listener, is himself, and is down to earth. One early college experience taught him a lot. He was in a limo for the first time and he and his boss were picking up F. Lee Bailey. His boss asked him if he wanted a drink. He politely declined. Then his boss said, "Alan, at the risk of offending you, let me tell you that it only costs a little more to go first class." And then he laughed.

Alan recalls, "Imagine what kind of moment in life that was for me. I had come all the way from a place where the grass was three or four feet tall out in the prairie on the other side of the tracks, all the way into one of the most successful, prominent plaintiff's attorneys who has ever walked this planet talking to me about it only costing a little more to go first class. That's going from one end of the socioeconomic spectrum to the other. To me, it was about breaking into a place where I was going to have to choose a fork in the road. Was I going to go down the path where I pour everything into being successful and having it be all about me? Or was I going to go down the other path, which seemed to me to be the one that I was groomed for from as far back as I could remember? I found myself smack dab in the middle of the socioeconomic system that I had always been dedicated to trying to change to help the have-nots. That second fork was not about being personally successful. It was about whether I would use the opportunities and influences in this socio-economic world to be of value. I told myself not to worry about being merely successful, but instead to focus on being valuable, and leaving things better than what I, and the people I lived with in my neighborhood, had experienced. I had a chance to make a meaningful difference. I had gotten all the way from there to here, and my future could be about having a limo and having a $7,000 tailored suit, or it could be about me using my opportunities and talents to make a difference for others."

Alan has devoted his life to learning and coaching, especially with the game of baseball and youth. He says he tries to teach them the value of what he calls an "ever-improving best effort." Alan explains, "For example, we don't worry so much about whether we are going to win or lose as much as we concern ourselves with doing our level best to become our best, and to make a point to step outside our comfort zones. When we do step outside our comfort zones, it is a healthy, good thing to try to do. But like any human, there would be a natural tendency to be fearful or afraid—afraid of failure, afraid of not measuring up, or afraid of being laughed at."

Alan feels that stepping outside of your comfort zone is a healthy thing because that is where the growth happens. He says, "Growth doesn't happen in the harbor where things are calm and safe. It happens when you step into situations where things aren't safe. When we step outside our comfort zone, we don't let things that we can't control interfere with the things that we can. If you were placed in a little dinghy and dropped into tumultuous waters, and you were trying to get across such a body of water like an ocean in these conditions, you would not allow yourself to be distracted by all of the tumultuous waves and everything that is going on outside of the boat, but rather you would pay attention to what is going on inside the dinghy and pay attention to which direction it is pointed and if you can get there from here. You don't let the things that you don't know interfere with the things you do know. You just try to look for signs of whether you are going in the right direction or the wrong direction, and believe me, I've run into plenty of brick walls where I realized that maybe this was not the direction I was supposed to be going. We are not put here to have accolades heaped on us or to just passively experience life, but rather we were put here to try our best to be part of the solution, and to be respectful, and to take time to understand other people's points of view along the way."

# Maximize Your Opportunities

*Kathleen Hopkins*

When you meet Kathleen Hopkins, you'd never know she was born in an Army base in the middle of Missouri with a hole in her heart. In fact, she didn't even know about it until she was forty-two years old. She says, "We have this big Irish Catholic family who is overbearing and over-competitive with each other. When we were growing up, we would never do anything that would prevent us from being Miss America. I thought I was just being a weenie for not being able to catch my breath; I was out of shape, and I should just do it harder, so I did." Growing up, her unknown defect didn't stop her from living out a well-rounded childhood, full of kayaking, running, biking, and any other outdoor activities she could endure.

She says, "I was just part of a large family of five girls and a boy; I'm the oldest and we were competitive with each other. There's a twelve-year span between the oldest and the youngest. Everybody, except maybe for one sister, is in really good physical fitness shape." Kathleen also strived to be well-rounded in her education—after undergrad, she was set to pursue her MBA when a professor stopped her and said she should go to law school instead. "As a woman with a glass ceiling, if you're not comfortable, you have a built-in business you can create. It's something for you to think about what your business is going to be."

Kathleen moved away from her big Irish Catholic family in New Jersey so that she could have more time to do outdoor activities. She took her husband along for the ride to University of Washington where she earned her law degree. "We moved to Seattle, and we were the black sheep for being all the way across the country. Of my mom's fourteen grandchildren two of them are in Seattle; the other twelve are in New Jersey within two or three towns of her."

Kathleen's career started moving immediately after law school, and her family started growing as well. Suddenly, she had a teenager who was having some trouble at school, and she realized the brunt of the burden was falling solely on her husband. "I felt I needed to be around more and decided to change my practice over to stop doing litigation. It was good timing because I wanted to have more control over my life, and I decided that control was more important than money and having control over my schedule and which cases or work I did was much more important to me than having a big paycheck and working long hours." She transitioned into a medium-sized firm where she worked as a "deal" lawyer.

Incredibly, that move may have saved her life. She was rallying her partners to get them the best possible individual disability policies they could, which required them to undergo physicals. "They said I had a heart murmur, and I needed to get an echocardiogram before they would insure me to make sure there was no problem with my heart. I'm like, 'What are you talking about? I have low blood pressure. I have low cholesterol, low heart rate.' Like any good lawyer, I argued with him for a few months and finally I called my doctor."

Even then, she was hesitant to realize what was standing right in front of her. When the doctors explained the problem with her heart, she was almost convinced he was wrong, or there was possibly another Kathleen Hopkins she was being confused with. It wasn't until the doctor placed a stethoscope in Kathleen's ears, aimed it at his own heart, and then at Kathleen's heart, that she began to accept what was happening.

Immediately, Kathleen was all business. "The one thing that I decided as a coping mechanism was that I had to treat this like any other business issue—make a plan and deal with it." Unfortunately, timing was not on Kathleen's side. While she was preparing for heart surgery, she was also in the midst of starting a new project at work and preparing her hometown of Seattle for an upcoming ABA meeting, including planning programs and parties. She pushed off the surgery until the last minute. "I figured if I was not going to live, if I died on the table, I was going to live as long as I could before I actually had the surgery because, why not? Why would you have the surgery one minute earlier than you needed to? Maybe they will find out they made a mistake in the meantime or there is something else they can do," she reasoned.

Finally, Kathleen had open-heart surgery. Despite a staph infection necessitating a second surgery, and a painful healing process, she got back to working and living as soon as she could drag herself out of bed. "After this surgery, I started running again, and I was feeling great." But soon, she found herself slowing down again; feeling pain where she shouldn't. She tried to blow it off as being out of shape, but eventually she knew she had to go back to the doctor. They found that her chest hadn't fully healed together at the bottom because of her infection. They ended up having to go back in and repair the valve they had placed into her heart. The doctors weren't able to save the initial valve and had to replace it with a new metal valve, which caused another staph infection. "I had separated myself mentally from this. I wanted to get back to work."

Kathleen could have thrown a pity party, or even just taken some well-deserved time off. Instead, she found gratitude. "Everything has been a blessing so far. I could have just dropped dead like other runners do." Only two weeks after her second surgery, tragedy struck when Kathleen's father passed away suddenly. He remains an inspiration to her today and she constantly strives to make him proud. But her saga still wasn't over.

In May 2006, Kathleen had a third open-heart surgery, during which the doctors remounted the inside of one of the chambers of her heart. "I was very annoyed because I had planned all this stuff for ABA Day for the Renaissance in the Profession." Three surgeries in, and Kathleen was still putting the ABA ahead of herself. She continued to plan her health around her engagements, rather than the other way around. Fortunately, she healed from her third surgery much more quickly than the other two.

Kathleen's health, her family issues, and her father's death hit her hard though. "I did everything right. It's not fair. I did everything right. I was not one of those old guys sitting in the waiting room who has been chain smoking and was fifty pounds overweight. I was exactly the perfect weight, my BMI was right on target, and this should not have been happening to me."

Currently, Kathleen doesn't have a solid prognosis, which is "driving me absolutely bonkers." She and her doctors continue to plan as best they can for the future, but nothing is as tangible as Kathleen would like it to be. "Of course, I'm worried about how long I'm going to be able to do it. I want to do stuff, but I can't. I've always been about maximizing an opportunity. I think that is probably my motto in life, so I wasn't going to go on the Board of Governors and just be a bum. I was going to go on the Board of Governors, join three committees, and do a task force because I was going to make a difference. I always want to make a difference and maximize an opportunity."

In the ABA, maximizing opportunities means finding a way to get people to do more *pro bono* projects, to make a difference again. She says, "We've been doing this project with Kids in Need of Defense (KIND) and it's a program to represent unaccompanied children in immigration proceedings. Right now, there are tens of thousands of children a year who go through immigration proceedings unrepresented."

It seems clear to me that while Kathleen doesn't have full control over her health or her body, she's channeling that need for power into making big things happen elsewhere. Her heart is always near the top of her mind, but she refuses to let herself become a slave to it. "Don't kill yourself by over-worrying about everything and over-analyzing everything but put it in perspective like you would any business situation or else you're not going to be able to function. This can eat up your entire life. You can just sit there worrying about it all day long, but if you're worrying about it all day long, you're not living your life. On the other hand, if I'm sitting there worrying about it all, then I've wasted time. I've wasted time that I should be living. Let go, focus on the big things, and don't worry so much."

Kathleen is refreshingly aware and honest of her need for control. But deep down, she's still a perpetual optimist, which I love. Her health forces her to keep the small stuff in perspective. She continues to work like there's no tomorrow. And, she believes in miracles. "Appreciate the waiter, the person who is holding the door open for you. Don't just appreciate your partner at the law firm or the client who is giving you a check but appreciate the secretary just as much as the cleaning woman. Maximize opportunities and be grateful and appreciate everybody."

# Practice Law with Passion

*Talmage Boston*

Growing up, Talmage Boston's heroes weren't superheroes, they were trial lawyers. "I was born in 1953 and the reason that's important is because I went to grade school in the early 1960s. During that time, there were two important events. One, America was celebrating the centennial of the Civil War and there was a lot of information being talked about in grade school, TV documentaries, children's books, and even trading cards—all on the subject of the Civil War. Obviously, the greatest hero of the Civil War was Abraham Lincoln. At a very young age, I had quite a fascination for all things Lincoln and, among other things, I realized that he had been a lawyer and I wanted to grow up to be like Abraham Lincoln, so I decided to be a lawyer. The second important event was the book *To Kill a Mockingbird* that came out in 1960. The movie came out on Christmas Day in 1962. I saw the movie shortly after it came out with my parents. I was nine years old and to see Atticus Finch in a courtroom, being a force against injustice was quite overwhelming. I wanted to grow up and be like Atticus Finch and I wanted to grow up and be like Abraham Lincoln."

He had a real-life mentor too, in that his father's brother, Charles Boston, who was an emerging young litigation partner at Fulbright, Crooker, Freeman, Bates & Jaworski (later shortened to Fulbright & Jaworski). His heroes inspired him to start public speaking at a young age. Talmage says, "In grade school I always liked to give speeches, do show and tell; I liked being on my feet and speaking, and I liked arguing." In third grade, Talmage read a biography of Thomas Jefferson and learned that Jefferson, like Talmage, loved arguing from a young age.

"He grew up and began his career as a lawyer, so I said to myself, 'Well, I guess that's what I'm supposed to become.'"

Besides being a big fan of both Abraham Lincoln and Atticus Finch, Talmage Boston is a big baseball fan. If you ever get the chance, sit down and pick his brain on the sport—he's not the type of person to throw clichés or baseball analogies at you like he's the first person to think of them—he has a unique perspective on the game that can be applicable to life, to the law, or to your practice.

This is one of my favorites: "Baseball is the only major team game that is not played against the clock. What that means is you have time between pitches to reflect on what's going on, and it's a great game for conversation with whoever you go to the game with. You talk about what's going on and why they did this and why they didn't do that, etc. I think that's a big part of the appeal. I think the main thing is that the pace of baseball leads to more reflection and more conversation."

But how does this apply to lawyering? As Talmage puts it, "Reflection and communication are equally important to the business of lawyering. No one in this profession will go far without being a good thinker and communicator."

To Talmage, baseball is more than just a sport. "Baseball has been the most incredible door-opener, whether it's John Grisham or David Brooks of *The New York Times* who was once our guest speaker at the 2009 Bar Convention here in Dallas. I connected with John and David through baseball." Having the ability to leverage a sport or activity you love, like baseball, into making business and even personal connections is a trait to be admired.

Talmage is a big baseball guy, but he's a lot more than that. After graduating from the University of Texas Law School in spring 1978, he went to work for the Dallas firm of Shank Irwin. "Their claim to fame was that they represented the first family of H.L. Hunt, Bunker Hunt, Hunter Hunt, Margaret Hunt Hill, Lamar Hunt." Then, in 1980, the silver market crashed. "The Hunts went from being the richest people in the world to having to file for bankruptcy. But that was a real education about how clients can go from good things to bad things in a very short period of time." After fifteen months of working on the Hunts' silver matter, Talmage became ready for a more diverse litigation practice and joined Payne, Spradley & Vendig, which had as its main client H.R. "Baum" Bright. In a short period of time, the firm went from eight to twenty-five and "everything was great." Then the S&L crisis hit and the firm's big S&L client, Bright Banc, was taken over by the federal government. "I again saw how economic fortunes can change very quickly." Talmage stayed with the firm for eight years after that, then went to Winstead in 1997 where he stayed until late 2017, when he moved his practice to the Dallas office of Shackelford, Bowen, McKinley & Norton, LLP. He's been board certified by the Texas Board of Legal Specialization in civil trial law since 1988 and civil appellate law since 1990, and he does business litigation, both trial and appellate. Starting out as a young lawyer during such a tumultuous economic climate, Talmage quickly learned that "Business is fragile; law firms are fragile; and don't ever think you're bulletproof."

Through his experience over his four decades as a lawyer, Talmage has been able to put into practice the lessons he's learned through his experience. "It's all about integrity. What goes around comes around. Your reputation is going to be a big part of how you're perceived, and it better be good, or you will suffer the consequences."

Talmage served on the State Bar of Texas board of directors from 2011 to 2014, and feels that the state bar not only does great things for the profession, but it's a great network to be a part of, too. He says, "Service in the bar association gives you a statewide network. I know lawyers all over the state who I can call, who I can trust, and who will be my local counsel or can help me evaluate things when I'm against a lawyer I don't know. I can get the lowdown on the lawyer, or if I'm in front of an unfamiliar judge I can make a call and find out what I need to know. It's just a fantastic network of people who I can trust and can give me information about their particular geographic area. That's a great thing to have at your fingertips."

The key to his stellar reputation? "You better practice law with a high level of passion and integrity because that's what clients want and expect, and that's how a professional establishes his or her reputation. Passion and integrity are the keys for a lawyer to create a great career, and they need to go hand-in-hand."

# Surround Yourself with Good People and Good Things Will Happen

*Hon. Jennifer Rymell*

Jennifer lives in Fort Worth, Texas, and is a former chair of the ABA Solo, Small Firm & General Practice Division who has lived much of her life without the existence of a comfort zone. Born in Dayton, Ohio, her family didn't stay in one place long enough during Jennifer's childhood for her to ever develop that sense of being from somewhere. At age four, Jennifer's father moved to Houston to pursue his PhD at Rice University. At age five, Jennifer moved with her mother to her grandparents' house in Fort Wayne, Indiana, where she started kindergarten. "I remember that as being a really happy time; I loved my grandparents; I loved my kindergarten." At Christmas of that year, Jennifer's father came back to Fort Wayne and convinced her mother to move the whole family to Houston with him. "We ended up moving to Houston, which was pretty unpleasant at first. Number one, my mother was very homesick. Number two, she had never driven on a freeway before; she didn't even know what a freeway was like."

But even more problematic, "She had never seen a roach before." Their first apartment lasted all of two days. "We broke the lease and had to find someplace else. My mom refused to live there." Starting in kindergarten, Jennifer attended three schools over four grades and lived in three different apartments. In fourth grade, she moved into a rental house in Illinois. In sixth grade, she changed school districts and attended a Catholic school. In seventh grade, she moved back to Houston. "My dad loved the climate in Houston; he got used to it; then all of a sudden, here he was back in the snow. Actually, my mom had gotten used to Houston by the time we left, and she liked the weather, too." Jennifer's family eventually purchased a house in Kingwood, just outside of Houston and her parents still reside there today.

About moving so much at such a young age, Jennifer recalls, "It was tough for me. I was a chunky kid growing up. Being a little overweight and being the new kid in school made it difficult to make friends. I always felt like I had to work extra hard to try to make friends and I think that is what made me more outgoing in the long run. I never had a comfort zone. After a year or two, we would move someplace else."

Her junior year of high school, her family moved to Holland. Her father was offered the opportunity to be an exchange scientist for Royal Dutch Shell in The Hague. "We were trading places with a scientist from the Hague. He was coming to Houston and he and his family were moving into our house and we were moving into their house. Jennifer always tells people, "I cried all the way there while we were on the plane. I'm a warm-weather girl. I get out of the plane and its 50-some degrees in July. It is gray, rainy, and cold, and I just cried and cried." But as soon as school started, that all changed.

"Everybody was extremely friendly because everybody knew what it was like to move around a lot and they knew they were at the school for only a certain period of time, and I loved the kids there. I had the best time." Holland brought Jennifer out of her shell. Not only did she meet her first love, she found her passion, and the career path she would begin to pursue shortly thereafter.

Jennifer's first boyfriend was the American ambassador's son. "The ambassador was a lawyer and that's how I decided I wanted to be a lawyer." Her time abroad was eye-opening, and she started leaning toward pursing international law, just as the ambassador had done. "I wanted to be an ambassador someday." After only a year in Holland, Jennifer came back to the states with a clear plan in mind. She said to herself, "'I want to graduate this year. I want to get into college and study political science. I want to go to law school.' That is what formed my whole future."

After taking and retaking the SAT, Jennifer was on her way. She knew her strengths, and she knew her weakness—math. "I used to think to myself, 'I am the daughter of a man who has a PhD in physics, and I cannot add.' I remember going through the catalog and looking for what seemed kind of 'law-ish,' where I don't have to take math, and I found criminal justice. I said, 'Okay, that sounds kind of like the law.'" After graduating magna cum laude from Southwest Texas State, Jennifer started law school at St. Mary's, where she is a distinguished alumnus today.

But, as she learned from her youth, nothing stays the same for long. "Even though I wanted to be an international lawyer and I wanted to live overseas, I started thinking about it. When I actually realized what international lawyers do by taking one international law class, I realized that was not for me." Instead, she pursued criminal law. And she got married. Her then husband was busy building his medical practice in Fort Worth, so Jennifer started looking for ways to fill her time. She got involved with the local League of Women Voters, she went to candidate school and learned how to moderate debates, and she became a co-host of a local cable television show. As she continued to moderate, she learned of an upcoming opening for city judge. At thirty years old, only five years out of law school, she applied and got the job.

As a municipal court judge, Jennifer soon realized that the job suited her well. "I felt like I had the temperament for it." She helped create the first truancy court for the city of Fort Worth. An opportunity arose for her to run for a county judge position and she says, "When you see an opportunity, you need to take it. Timing is everything in life."

Jennifer took the opportunity and found success. She was elected to the bench and took office in 2003, and "my life changed in 2005 because I got pregnant and I had Dylan. I found myself with an 18-month-old and now I was getting divorced. That was definitely a defining moment in my life because I had this little person who was completely helpless, and I was his lifeline. I loved him more than I have ever loved anything in my life. I said to myself, "Nobody is an island. Surround yourself with good people and good things are going to happen."

Jennifer continued her career and learned how to readjust and balance. It wasn't an immediate transition. She says, "I really saw at an early time in my career the difference that bar association work can make, not only in the lives of lawyers, but more importantly in the lives of the public. It's a selfish thing, but it feels good to make such a difference." After a long history in the state bar and the Texas Young

Lawyers Association, she became chair of the Solo, Small Firm & General Practice Division and is now a delegate to the House of Delegates of the ABA.

She eventually married again to Chuck Noteboom, a successful trial lawyer in Fort Worth. "Super mom. Super lawyer. Super extracurricular person. We either have a passion for community service or bar service and we're supposed to fire on all cylinders." The first few years of her son's life, Jennifer admits she stretched herself too thin. She had to pull back from some of her passions, and she did. But she persevered, and soon she was back to hitting new goals. "I learned how to give time to my career and still give time to my love of the law, loving my bar association work, but then taking care of Dylan." It's a constant question among women, especially those who know the challenge of balancing a career and a family—how does she do it? "I relied heavily on my family and friends." Jennifer told me a motto she learned from one of her best friends, who had heard it from another partner at her firm: "You can have it all, but you can't have it all at the same time." Jennifer is one of the best friends a girl can have and she certainly hits it right on point in my book.

# Speak up When Something's Not Right

*Michael S. Greco*

---

Michael Greco was born in Rende, a small village in southern Italy, during World War II. His father was a native Italian and his mother was a US citizen born in Chicago. The couple met when Michael's mother and her mother took a trip to Italy. They fell in love, and married in 1937. "My mother's dream was always to go back to the US to raise the family." That dream was realized after the war, in October of 1950 when Michael, age 7; his parents; and four siblings arrived at Ellis Island in New York Harbor. He still remembers vividly his first sighting of the Statue of Liberty and his first steps on US soil with a sense of awe and gratitude.

After living for several months in Baltimore, Maryland, at the home of Michael's maternal grandfather, who had picked them up at Ellis Island (his maternal grandmother had passed away shortly after Michael's birth in 1942), the family moved to Chicago, and in 1952 moved to the suburb of Hinsdale, Illinois, where the family settled and Michael attended public school. "I was very open to the new adventure and had such a great excitement level to be meeting my grandfather, my mother's father, and other family members. In the village of Rende I had never seen a person of color. I did not know what prejudice was. I had never been aware of bigotry or people being mean to other people. In America I soon learned the meaning and ugliness of bigotry and prejudice. To my disappointment and sadness, I came to realize that my grandfather was bigoted. He discriminated, and he thought and said things about people of color that deeply bothered me."

One of Michael's first hard lessons in life was how to deal with prejudice when it is demonstrated by a family member, especially one's grandfather. "Even if it is someone you love, when he or she shows lack of respect for human beings you have to decide what to do about it." Michael, at age 8, had a difficult conversation with his grandfather, asking many questions. He could not accept the answers given. "That experience set me on an early path that helped to shape my values growing up and define the person I wanted to be, and did not want to be. That path eventually led to my reasons to become a lawyer, to choices I made during my legal career, and ultimately to my priorities as president of the American Bar Association and later chair of the ABA Center for Human Rights, among other ABA activities. The experience with my grandfather ingrained in me the belief that when I recognized a wrong, especially harm to human beings, even if committed by a family member, friend, or person I respect, I have to do something about it."

In the fall of 1952, shortly after moving from Chicago to the suburb of Hinsdale, Michael, then in fourth grade, had his first experience with being an advocate, a precursor to his career as a trial lawyer. His family had moved into their new home in September for the start of the school year, and the fall days were unseasonably cold. But the utilities had not yet been connected to the home nor were they connected for more than a week thereafter. His thirty-six-year-old father was frustrated because his command of English didn't allow him to explain to the Hinsdale town officials what the problem was. "My father asked me to go with him to the town hall to meet with the town manager (mayor) and explain the conditions under which we were living—no running water, electricity or heat—and why it was important that the utilities finally be connected. As we sat across the town manager's big desk I described the situation, and ended by politely asking how he and his family would like to live in their house for a week without water, electricity, and heat on cold nights, with no help in sight. He replied that he would not like it at all. He apologized, and said that all the utilities would be installed the next day. They were. So my very first advocacy effort, at age 9, was on behalf of my brothers and sisters and parents.

The incident proved lessons learned for me. One was the importance of speaking up and taking action when something is not right. You have to help—you cannot take a pass. Too many people regrettably do take a pass. Another was about the serious obstacles that immigrants face when they don't know the language, don't know the procedures, and don't know how to get things done. They don't know what to do or to whom to turn. The advocacy experience also informed me that I had enjoyed helping to solve a problem. The experience and similar others as I grew up eventually led me to become a lawyer in order to solve problems facing people who needed but had no help. Those early lessons are reflected in the initiatives I chose to implement as president of the American Bar Association in 2005–06."

As Michael and his family adjusted to life in America and the Chicago area, he grew into a fairly typical American boy. "I had an after-school job in a neighborhood mom-and-pop grocery store from fifth grade until twelfth grade. At night I worked hard on my studies. I played three varsity sports. In my senior year I was fortunate to be awarded to get a modest ($800) academic scholarship named the Rodney Kroehler Award, annually awarded to a graduating scholar-athlete. Princeton University also granted me an academic scholarship (there were no athletic scholarships in the Ivy League). Summer and campus jobs helped to pay the balance of the tuition."

During high school, Michael became immersed in issues of equality, or the lack thereof, throughout America's history. He credits a progressive, white, young Hinsdale High School teacher, Benjamin Nelson, born and raised in Mississippi who went north to teach, for being a guiding light. The course was American History, taken in Michael's junior year, in 1959. "The decision of what I would do with my life became very clear to me in that class. When we read about the Civil War period, and participated in class discussions about slavery, and how it divided and almost tore the country apart. Mr. Nelson told the class about the answer that President Abraham Lincoln gave to the question why he, born and raised in the south, had never been a slave owner. 'As I would not be a slave, I shall not be a slave owner.' That phrase has been in my mind ever since I first heard it. I learned in that American History course law is the equalizer. I learned that the US Constitution is a magnificent document, and that, in simplest terms, the underlying purpose of the Constitution in America's democracy is to protect the weak from the strong, to protect the minority view from the majority. At age 16, I decided, 'That is what I want to do. That is what I will do.'"

After serving as president of the ABA, Michael was invited by the chief judge of the US district court in Boston to deliver keynote remarks at a naturalization ceremony, held at the John F. Kennedy Presidential Library, to a group of 200 new US citizens. He said to them, "You and I have something in common. I came to this country as a boy of seven years, many of you have come to America later in life. We are now American citizens. As time passes you may not remember much of what I say to you today. If you remember nothing else, please remember this: It does not matter whether someone has been an American citizen for only one generation or ten generations. Everyone in this country except the American Indian is either an immigrant or a descendant of an immigrant. Immigrants have helped to build this great country from the time the colonists first immigrated to America from England 250 years ago to escape persecution and start a new and better life. Immigrants will continue to help build America. Never forget that. You have as much a right as anyone else to work hard, to raise your family, to contribute and to vote to help shape this country and its values."

In his remarks Michael also urged the new Americans to stay informed and be current about the government, our elected officials, and the decisions made by those in elected office. He urged them to always exercise the precious right to vote, and to embrace and honor the important responsibilities that come with US citizenship, to perform civic duties, to become leaders in the community. "'Exercising the right to vote is the only way that necessary changes happen in this country. Too many people are now indifferent or uneducated about the many rights guaranteed in our Constitution, too many people do not exercise the right to vote, and too many are silent and inactive when they know that something is deeply wrong and unacceptable. Do not be that way. Have courage.'"

To illustrate, he uses an example from the end of his year as ABA president. It was a year during which President George W. Bush by executive order had implemented a number of policies during the War on Terror, such as spying on private citizens, authorizing the torture of captured enemy soldiers, using "presidential signing statements" to refuse to execute laws adopted by Congress, among other policies. The ABA president appointed task forces comprised of bi-partisan, expert, constitutional scholars to determine whether the Bush Administration policies violated the Constitution. The reports issued by the task forces unanimously concluded that they did. The ABA House of Delegates thereupon adopted resolutions urging the president to revoke his unconstitutional policies. The policies were not revoked. In his last major speech as ABA president, in July 2006, at the Commonwealth Club in San Francisco, Michael forcefully addressed the Bush Administration's harmful policies, basing his remarks on the forceful responses of the American Bar Association's House of Delegates that urged the president to cease the violations, and on other policies adopted historically by the American Bar Association. He urged the American people to speak up, to express firmly their strong opposition to erosion of their constitutionally protected rights, to protect vigorously their freedoms, to exercise their right to vote. The speech was broadcast live on radio on the West Coast, and on tape the following week on the East Coast.

A young mother of two girls aged five and seven happened to turn on her car radio as she was driving on a California highway and she started to listen to the live broadcast. She did not know who was speaking and she kept listening. Her eyes started to tear up at what she was hearing, so she pulled off the highway and parked her car to finish listening to the broadcast. In the following days she tried to learn who had delivered the speech. She learned it was the president of the American Bar Association. She wrote and sent a letter to the ABA headquarters in Chicago, which Michael received weeks later, and to which he responded. The letter expressed the great fear and worry felt by the young mother about the kind of world in which her young daughters would live, and gratitude for the "courageous remarks" about Americans protecting their precious freedoms that she had heard on the radio. At the end of her letter she quoted Rosalynn Carter—"A leader takes people where they want to go. A great leader takes people where they don't necessarily want to go, but ought to be"—and commented, "That's what you are trying to do. Please do not stop."

After serving as president of the American Bar Association, Michael returned to his law firm practice and he has continued his efforts to take people "where they ought to be" through his work within and without the ABA, including as chair for the ABA Center for Human Rights and chair of the ABA International Criminal Court Project, as a visiting professor teaching in China international criminal law and human rights, and other public interest activities. Michael's career has come full circle. "I came to America in 1950 at age seven not knowing how to speak English, knowing nothing about American culture and society, meeting my grandfather for the first time and learning from him about, and then coming to grips with, bigotry and racism and violations of human dignity and human rights. During my forty-five year career as a lawyer I have tried to use my legal skills to confront the injustices that I learned about as a boy, and many others that I have confronted since then. I have no intention of stopping."

Michael S. Greco has lived the advice that he has given to others: "Speak Up When Something's Not Right."

# Speak Truth to Power

*Leslie H. Lowe*

My dear friend, the late Leslie Lowe and I first bonded over Nancy Drew. Leslie says, "Nancy Drew was smart and spunky. She taught us about influence and feminism." We both love strong women with a head on their shoulders—and having her own roadster didn't hurt.

Leslie was my first African American friend and I met her in Paris in 1976 where, after winning Dick Clark's $25,000 Pyramid Show, she moved to Paris to get her second master's degree in African History from the Sorbonne. Leslie was one of the most intelligent, strongest women I ever had the joy of knowing. She grew up with a mother and stepfather who were both lawyers and was bitten by the law bug at an early age. Her mother, the late Judge Mary Lowe, was the second African American and female federal judge appointed by President Carter. I learned so much from her being the skinny, eighteen-year-old, wet-behind-the-ears Texan I was.

In education, her family was ahead of the curve—her mother was a second-generation college graduate. She says, "It was expected that we would go to college. There was no question about it. The thought of not finishing high school wasn't even on the agenda. People talk about the 'talented tenth' among black people. There was a segment of the black population that was educated, and I came from an educated family."

Leslie never expected to become an environmental lawyer, but it's easy to see where the inspiration for her career started. During her formative years, Leslie attended a Lutheran summer camp in northeastern Pennsylvania.

"There was an incredible rhododendron forest that had grown over a dry creek bed. There were all these flat stones that we could play on. It was our playhouse." Leslie loved her summer camp, she loved going on hikes, and she learned the importance of not littering and leaving places better than she found them. "You should put back more than you took out. I think if we all take more than we give there is nothing left for anybody." Her childhood led to her to find joy whenever she was able to have a beautiful, natural place to spend time in. This experience paid off in later years when she fought to save the public park areas in New York City.

Leslie graduated Harvard Law School in 1980, when the foundation for globalization of the World Trade Organization was being built. She started working in the tax department at Sherman & Sterling. "I worked on a major international arbitration in the bank finance department. Again, because of my political perspective, which is decidedly to the left, I was very skeptical about much of what I did and saw. When I left, I went to work for an organization at that time which was called The Lawyers Committee for International Human Rights."

To set the scene, this was shortly after the murder of The Maryknoll Sisters nuns—three American missionaries in El Salvador. The Lawyers Committee represented the families of the women who were murdered. Leslie worked primarily on the Haitian refugee crisis. She says, "I worked with people who were here in the US preparing the refugees for their silent applications. I worked with the late Arthur Helton, who was one of the outstanding figures in the human rights field. Because I spoke French, they sent me to the Human Rights Convention in Geneva."

Leslie also worked for the New York Appellate Division, where she first started learning about environmental law. "I said, 'Judge, I don't have to do the criminal cases. I'll do all the environmental and land use cases.' And that was fine with him." She worked on a lot of cases in which a government real estate action required an environmental review. When David Dinkins was elected mayor, Leslie had a colleague who was named head of the Department of General Services, a quasi-business agency for the city. "He became commissioner and asked me to become assistant commissioner and work for him. I left the court and did that." Leslie became an expert in the city charter, focusing much of her work on land issues and due process regarding land procurement. "Later in my career, I learned how government works, how the process works. When I left the city, I did some consulting work. At some point, a friend called and asked what I was doing, and I said that I didn't know yet. He said, there's this organization that is looking for somebody. It was the New York City Environmental Justice Alliance."

Eventually, Leslie left working the city. Shortly thereafter, she was approached by a woman named Cindy Worley, who asked her if she would represent an organization *pro bono* called the New York City Community Garden Coalition. She says, "Of course, my first inclination was to say, 'Are you kidding me?' But she started telling this very compelling story, and I knew about the community gardens because I lived downtown, Lower Manhattan, and I could see the gardens here and there, and they were really very nice. I was shocked that the city, again, this was under Giuliani, was starting to close them and sell the land."

Leslie became an advisor to the gardens and ultimately became involved in the litigation. The issue became widely publicized throughout the city, and eventually Giuliani said the city was going to auction off all of the gardens. "Pete Seeger came to publicize the fate of the gardens, and on the eve of the auction, Bette Midler came through with enough money to buy the gardens. She just said, 'Here, I'll take these.' She bought about half of them. Some of the land trust groups came up with the money and bought the other half. That's what saved the community gardens. There had been interim litigation that by the New York State Attorney General and they got a stay on some of the community gardens. That's how we saved New York City's Community Gardens."

It is amusing how a city girl would become such an advocate for the environment. That irony was not lost on Leslie. She says, "Even though I lived most of my life in New York City, I've always cared very deeply about the natural world. That comes from my childhood experiences—spending my summers in the mountains at summer camp—and just having a beautiful, natural place to play in. I think kids today are so deprived because all of their play is so supervised. They have play dates and are not allowed to just run out into the woods and explore nature and find salamanders."

Leslie also saw gardens as an important part of the melting pot that is New York City. During the 1970s a gardening movement started taking hold in the city—she saw how the community gardens were knit together by neighbors hailing from the Caribbean, Asia, Latin America, and from everywhere. "That is also part of the culture of New York

City. We're an immigrant city. Each of these groups brings something to the city," she said with passion and commitment.

Leslie learned how to be a powerful lawyer by protecting the gardens and the environment from the big city machine. "Every time you dare to speak truth to power, every time you voice an opinion that is not received or accepted opinion, that's a defining moment. My defining moments have been largely those moments where I saw that something was important but didn't necessarily have powerful defenders or articulate defenders was at risk. Like the gardens. The people in the community loved those gardens. By all rights, if tending something and taking care of it gave you ownership rights, those people owned those gardens. The city only neglected them. The real estate speculators would just buy them at auction and hold them for a while, and if they couldn't flip them for a profit, they'd let them become abandoned lots again."

Leslie continued to keep her voice while still fighting for the betterment of our world. She talked at length about how our economy is ultimately destructive of our environment. "We are not thinking forward." Leslie was always looking for incentives to fix our economy, fix our environment, and better our future. Her ultimate goal was to make the better choices also the rational ones. She wanted to see the government create economic incentives to tell the country to do the right thing.

As long as I knew her, she never gave up that fight, and she never stopped speaking about it. "I cherish the freedom I have to throw myself into something and work on it until either I realize I'm knocking my head against a stone wall, or until I'm satisfied that I've done everything that I could possibly do." Leslie was never afraid to speak her mind about what she saw as just and right. Her legacy lives on in the gardens of New York City and all the hearts and minds she touched in her too-short time on earth. And what she taught this Texan girl about being a good human being, taking risks and living your dreams will never be forgotten. The day we went to the Paris Marche aux Puces and tried to sell our necklaces before our store opened was a memory I will never forget. But the gendarmes never caught up with us!

# You Can Come Back from a Mistake

*Raquel "Rocky" A. Rodriguez*

Rocky's parents fled Cuba in 1959 when the Communists took over. Like out of a Dan Brown novel, her father sought asylum in the Honduran embassy. She says, "They left everything behind; my mother's family had been in the sugarcane business; my father's family also had a farm and my grandfather's pharmacy. They thought they would be here just for a small amount of time, so they didn't bring any of their personal effects." Two years into her parent's exile, Rocky was born. "Eventually, my father went into sales and continued in that the rest of his career." Although he was a lawyer in Cuba, he never pursued the career in the states. She says, "He never went into law because he would have had to start law school all over again, and he had to make money to support us."

However, her family's plight and father's forced career change shaped Rocky and her entire outlook on life. Rocky remembers, "I grew up always thinking of myself as an American first, but I always grew up very aware that I had my roots in Cuba, and that my family had lost everything, that democracy was good, and communism was bad. My father was very politically active in the Cuban exile community. I grew up going to political rallies, political meetings, and listening to discussions about how we invade Cuba, and how we get the US government to get rid of Castro. I grew up going to banquets. By the time I was going to young lawyers' events, the 'rubber chicken' circuit was old hat to me. I've been going to banquets since I was a kid."

Rocky was a star in both undergraduate and law school, where she pursued her dream of working in international litigation. After graduating she was personally offered a position at Greenberg Traurig by one of the founders. "I remember the day that I met Mel Greenberg. He has passed now but he was a very tall, striking-looking man with a mischievous little glint in his blue eyes. Speaking of people who had a major influence on my life, he was one of them. The first thing that Mel asked me when we met was 'So, are you a Democrat or a Republican?' And I said, 'I'm a Republican.' He goes, 'Oh, that's right. It's the Cuban thing.' I loved his humor."

Rocky reveled in her early career. "I felt like I got a really fast start, and I had really wonderful training to be working under the kind of lawyer who brought an associate to everything. I was there at every deposition and I was on every call, and I had a lot of responsibility. My first two years as a lawyer was an extended education by getting to do it." Mel Greenberg requested she be transferred to a special team formed to handle foreclosures. Although she went "kicking and screaming," she soon realized it was an excellent move for her because she says, "I became an expert in commercial foreclosure and banking litigation. In a short amount of time I had my own case load." Rocky adjusted quickly to the increased responsibility.

One of her most memorable defining moments came on the cusp of her growing success. In handling her first foreclosure from beginning to end, she made a mistake. "What I didn't realize was that you filed your foreclosure with whatever information you have and then when you get the title update, you amend it. I held on and held on and didn't file the claim. The client got upset and fired the firm from handling their foreclosures—because of me."

Rocky didn't learn the consequences of her inaction until her review, and then she became incredibly upset. "Mel used to manage by walking around and tapping on your office door to see what you were doing and to come in and talk to you. He came by one day and said, 'I heard that you had your evaluation and that you were very upset at the news of our client leaving the firm. Let me tell you something. There is not a lawyer in the world that has not lost a client, and any lawyer that tells you they have not, is lying. Take it as a lesson, learn from it and move on.' I learned in that moment that you can come back from a mistake. That when you make a mistake, you just have to move on."

Rocky moved right into the Young Lawyers Division of the ABA where she quickly became influential. "I learned a lot of skills in terms of leadership and teamwork, in terms of extending my views, and in terms of getting things done. I made the best friends I ever had through bar work. It was a very enriching time. One should go into it for the right reasons."

Her work with the ABA, where she acted as an ambassador for the Young Lawyers and for American lawyers for other country's bar associations, led her to her next job. At her first meeting of the Association of International Young Lawyers in Vichy, France, she met a fellow American and quickly befriended him. He introduced her two years later to her future job—in London! "How are you going to keep them on the farm after they've seen Paris?"

The offer to run Multilaw was an easy "yes" for Rocky, who felt she was finally living her dream of pursuing an international legal practice and getting to travel the world. But as much as Rocky felt at home in London, at the job of her dreams, life got in the way. Her mother's health was deteriorating, and after two years, Rocky ended up asking to be released. She told her news to the chairman of Greenberg Traurig, Larry Hoffman, who told her they were considering an international expansion. "I said, 'Oh, that's interesting.' We just started talking and we worked it out that I would come back to the firm and do for Greenberg what I had been doing for Multilaw, which was fine." It was a very sad time for her because Rocky's mother passed soon after. Rocky knew in her heart she had done her best to make her mother proud.

A mentor at Greenberg Traurig, Sue Cobb, led Rocky to an unexpected career change. She started volunteering on George W. Bush's presidential campaign. "My law firm later was hired for the 2000 election litigation, so I went from being a volunteer to working on the clock." She loved the pace, the excitement, learning how to work with different people and personalities, "I've never had a better time as a lawyer in my whole life." Months later, Rocky was offered a chance to apply to be general counsel to Governor Jeb Bush. She ended up not applying because she wanted to be able to financially help her father and did not want to leave her firm.

But again, life directed Rocky in the way she was meant to go. In 2002, following her father's remarriage, she moved to the Greenberg Washington office. She got a call from Jeb's general counsel. "He said,

'Hey, I heard you might be interested at some point in being general counsel to Governor Bush and he's just appointed me to the court of appeals. I have to find my replacement. Would you be interested in interviewing?' I said, 'Well, I wish you had called me a week ago; I just bought an apartment up here in Washington. When can I let you know?'"

Two weeks after Rocky interviewed with Jeb and was in Miami, she received a call from Jeb's assistant. She said, "'Oh, Rocky, hold on, the governor would like to speak with you.' He said, 'Rocky?' I said, 'Hello, governor.' He said, 'How would you like to be my general counsel?'"

We make plans, and God laughs. "The lesson there, between that and the Multilaw opportunity, was that those were not some of the big things that I set out to do. They just happened as I pursued other things that I loved. Some of the things that I had pursued ardently, like being a lawyer in London, or being an international corporate lawyer, those things just for whatever reason, they didn't work out exactly as I had intended. And better yet, while I was in the process of just doing things that I enjoyed, like bar association work or election volunteering, the things that were meant for me, found me. I always figured that when it's meant for you, the right opportunity will present itself."

# PART 3
# Authenticity

# Find Your Voice Because No One's Going to Give It to You

*Barbara Mayden*

Barbara never knew a lawyer growing up, but she was familiar with injustice. She had a civics teacher in junior high school who taught her class comparative political systems. "When I was in seventh or eighth grade, a parent hauled him into court for teaching communism. It was humiliating for him and horrifying to most of his students and me. It just didn't seem right that our justice system could subject somebody to this." After studying political science as an undergrad, Barbara decided to continue on into law school.

From there, she was hired as one of the very first women to join the firm of King & Spalding. Around the same time, the National Conference of Women in the Law was coming to Atlanta—until they weren't. "They announced they were not coming to Atlanta because Georgia was a non-ERA state. They were boycotting Atlanta. That was radicalizing because it seemed to me fairly basic that if any state needed a conference on women in the law, it would be a non-ERA state. That is what got me interested in being a leader on issues of how the law affected women and how we could use the law as an instrument for change. We were victorious. They did come to Atlanta, and I played a big part in that."

But it took a while for that victory to translate into Barbara's personal life. Back in those days there were many clubs that were for men only. As a young associate at King & Spalding, she recalled going to a meeting in Richmond, Virginia. "We had the meeting at the law office and we left to go to lunch.

We went to a private club in Richmond, and we were all going into the club when they said to me, 'Oh no. You can't go in with us. You've got to go in through the kitchen.' The men walked in the front door and I had to walk in through the kitchen. I was so young, it never occurred to me to say, 'I am not walking into the kitchen. This is wrong.'"

Another time, she went to New York to meet a group for a closing dinner, again at a private club. She got off the plane in her lawyer suit and went straight to the event with her suitcase. She was a little early. She says, "I told them I was there for the Goldman Sachs dinner. They told me that it didn't start until 7:30 and it was only 6:30." Despite it being freezing and snowing, she was told to wait outside because "unescorted women cannot wait in the club until a male shows up to escort them in." She says, "I asked if I looked like a prostitute to no avail. I stood outside in the snow waiting for the first man to show up."

In retrospect, Barbara knows this was wrong, and still to this day has a sense of discomfort about the whole thing. But the most bothersome thing, "Is that I didn't have the courage to confront them and say, 'What are you talking about?' Or just to leave. I knew it was wrong. I needed a voice. I needed to be able to establish some authority."

Another meeting rolled around, and Barbara was determined to change the way she, and other women in her workplace, were treated. At this point, she was about twenty-six years old, cute, thin, and people looked right through her. She says, "I thought, 'What can I do after this experience, so people don't do this?'" She walked into a room filled with twenty men and felt a wave of anxiety. The answer just came to her. She strode straight to the head of the table, and in her strongest and most confident voice she said, "'Gentlemen, let's get this meeting started.' I went and sat my rear end down at the head of the table. They stood up straighter and looked startled, but sat down. It just took that little bit of assertiveness to be taken seriously."

After that meeting, Barbara felt a huge shift in her professional life. "I realized that I had to be assertive because of my age and gender. I had to overcome the fear of feeling like I didn't know what the heck I was talking about; slowly realizing that nobody really knows what they're talking about and just talk anyway. You just do it."

I call it the "fake it 'til you make it" strategy. It works. Even when you are a seasoned lawyer, you face situations that are new and uncertain, and you just have to tackle it head-on and get the job done.

Ever since, Barbara has held on to her voice, and now helps young women lawyers find their own as well. She says, "You have to have the courage to just speak through the fear. Once you realize that we are all scared (most of us, there are some jerks who have the arrogance) it gets easier. Everybody, when they first start practicing law, is just terrified that they will be called out because they don't know what the heck they are doing. I remember sitting in my little office one day and I got a phone call. Apparently, they couldn't get hold of the partner. They said, 'Barbara, we've got you on the speaker, the entire group is here, and we have a question to ask you.' I thought, 'I'm supposed to answer this question?' That's terror. Real terror. Tears came to my eyes. But, once you find your voice, you learn that it's okay to say, 'That's a great question. Let me get back to you on that.' That is empowering. Nobody expects you to know everything and have the answer at the tip of your tongue. They appreciate you not trying to blow smoke. Then you figure it out. You learn to ask the right people for help."

Through her career, motherhood, and going back to work, she has been a constant advocate for women. She is a prolific public speaker with a great sense of humor. However, even finding her public speaking voice was a challenge for her. In law school, she had a terrible fear of public speaking. She first discovered her fear one day when she was called on in a large class. "My professor called on me to recite the facts of a case. In that class you had to stand up. Well as I stood up, simultaneously, my brain fell to my feet. I couldn't talk, and the professor kept saying 'Miss Mendel, are you okay?' I couldn't talk. I was so terrified I couldn't get a word out. It was excruciating."

Barbara wrote off public speaking as something that would never be in her skill set, but she was faced with her fear again during her young lawyer days. "A partner in my firm took me by the ear and told me I was going to an ABA Young Lawyers meeting." She took to it, and was later talked into running for chair of the Young Lawyers Division. She says, "Another friend of mine in the Young Lawyers Division, Mark Schickman from California, became sort of my personal mentor in public speaking."

Not too long into her tenure as chair, the ABA considered charging separate dues for membership in the Young Lawyers Division instead of making it automatic with joining the ABA. Barbara knew it would dramatically cut off the division's membership numbers. "Public speaking was excruciating for me until there was a huge issue affecting the Young Lawyers. It was a critical and empowering issue, and we had to rise up because we thought the issue impacted the viability of the Young Lawyers Division." Suddenly, Barbara had no choice but to stand up in front of the entire YLD assembly and "extemporaneously rally the troops." She did it. "It was off the top of my head. I did it—and learned I could do it. The passion I had for the issue was so intense, something so important, that I forgot I didn't know how to speak."

As she found her voice, Barbara felt she was finally in control of her own destiny. "Waiting for somebody to empower me wasn't going to cut it. It took going and sitting at the head of that table and saying, 'Gentlemen, let's get started' to take control of my career. Nobody could do that for me. What I'm trying to do now in my second career as a legal headhunter is help people who are miserable in their jobs say, 'I don't have to be miserable here. Is it the law I hate? No. It's my work setting that I don't like and it's up to me to do something about it.' That is very, very rewarding to me now."

# Be Transparent

*Hon. John V. Singleton, III*

---

The late Southern District of Texas Senior Chief Judge John Singleton was the definition of authenticity and transparency. A yellow dog Democrat from humble beginnings, he lived to the ripe old age of ninety-seven and played golf and worked in his office up to the very end. He shared offices with Richard "Racehorse" Haynes, another old friend of mine. His story exemplifies my belief that being authentic and transparent is always the best solution to any situation that confronts you. People have an innate radar that tells them when you are being truthful, and even when you feel most vulnerable, you may be at your most powerful. As lawyers, we tend to have the need to seem omnipotent to our clients, as if we can wave a magic wand and make all their problems go away. Sometimes we don't have all the answers, and often, that is the answer—just tell the truth and say, "I don't know. But here is what I will do to find a solution."

Judge Singleton was a federal judge appointed by President Lyndon Baines Johnson (LBJ). Judge Singleton's route to becoming a federal judge had a lot to do with the fact that he did not want to go to Dallas with President John F. Kennedy (JFK), who had just visited Houston the day before, on that fateful trip where Kennedy was assassinated in 1963.

He recalls, "Both Kennedy and Johnson wanted me to go to Dallas with them. I said no, and that I would see them in Austin the next night. Had I gone, my whole life would have been different. Lyndon relied on people that he liked. If he thought you were smart enough, he would do anything for you. It was a turning point for me because if I had gone to

Dallas, I might have gone straight to Washington and might not have become a federal judge. I said no to going because I had just taken off for about three weeks and, with the Secret Service, went through every hotel in town before Kennedy got here, and I organized the receiving line for him. In fact, I've got all this in a memo that I dictated after Governor John Connally got shot along with JFK. I was sitting in my office that day, and some guy came running in and said that both John Kennedy and John Connally had been shot and were dying. I was good friends with Gus Wortham, who had an airplane. I called him and told him that I wanted to go to Dallas. I took his plane and landed in Dallas as Air Force One was taking off for Washington. Bob Strauss and his wife met me at the airport. I was with Nellie Connally, John's wife, the day when they told her that John was going to live. Nellie asked me to dictate a memo about the events leading up to the situation. It says nearly everything I'm saying now, but more."

I am honored that Judge Singleton gave me the original of that memo on the day I interviewed him. It is a precious record of that historic visit John F. Kennedy had in Houston before he was assassinated in Dallas. My many years of friendship with Judge Singleton started in 1984 when I chaired the Law Day Committee for the Houston Young Lawyers Association. At that time, the annual Law Day naturalization ceremony was led by Judge Singleton in the federal courts. We worked on the Law Day luncheon together for three years. Former Attorney General Griffin Bell was our keynote speaker in 1984, James Baker spoke in 1985, and in 1986 then-Governor Mark White spoke on the third year. It was an honor and a lot of fun to work with Judge Singleton. His sense of humor and fun was always apparent.

Judge Singleton's career in public service started at a very young age. He said, "I guess another defining moment was when I was six years old. I had a used bicycle. I gave it to an orphan boy. I've always had a feeling for the underdog. I never was a liberal. In fact, people think I was a liberal, but I was not. The newspapers called me a populist, which I was. But I ended up doing a lot as a federal judge. I was the only Texas judge ever to be elected to the Judicial Conference of the United States."

The origins of his desire to be a lawyer were as unique as everything else about him. He says, "When I was a kid in Waxahachie, Dan Moody was governor of Texas. He had beaten Ma Ferguson in the late 1920s.

He was a friend of my father's, and he was a great lawyer. He was my idol and he wore a bow tie. I always said that if I ever got to become a lawyer, I was going to wear a bow tie, which I did. I always wanted to be lawyer, and surprisingly enough, in law school, my friends and I thought it would be great to be a federal judge. Federal judges, as you know, are appointed for life. At that time, federal judges were making $10,000 a year. And we used to say to each other, "Wouldn't it be wonderful to be a federal judge and have a salary for the rest of your life?"

Something that really stuck in the judge's craw was the fact that the Houston Bar Association was not integrated. His memory of that time was as sharp as a tack, "I took off for about three months to go to Atlantic City to work on the 1964 campaign for the Democratic Convention. In 1965 I was sitting in my office and the telephone rang. It was Lyndon. He said, 'John, did you know that Houston is the largest city in the United States where the bar isn't integrated?' I said, 'I knew that Mr. Johnson.' He said, 'Well, get off your rear end and do something about it.' The African Americans had their own bar association at that time. My law partner, George Barra, was president of the Houston Bar. I hung up the phone and said, 'George, I've just been told by the president of the United States that he wants the bar association integrated. He wants it done now.' Sure enough, we integrated the bar in 1966. Lyndon asked me to do it, and that's what I was going to do."

Some of the controversial cases the judge presided over drew publicity. There were times that he was in the paper every day. He is best known for his "hair cases." The judge said, "I had the first hair case in Texas, brought by Carlos Calbillo. San Jacinto Junior College kicked him out because he had a beard and a mustache. I wrote in my opinion about how sitting in my office I saw pictures of Oliver Wendell Holmes and William Blackstone, all of whom had long hair, beards, and mustaches."

One of Judge Singleton's toughest life challenges came in 1976, when he learned that the US Attorney wanted to indict him. He doesn't remember exactly what for, and he said he never knew why. But he got a letter from the US Attorney's office, which had contacted the chief judge of the Southern District and listed cases against banks in which he had loans. The US Attorney wanted to indict him on making false statements to get loans from banks, which he said he never did. At the time, he had several cases against banks in his court. He went to Austin, voluntarily, and was interviewed by the Federal Bureau of Investigation for two days. His lawyer, Mark Susman, who was a former US attorney, went with him. After that, they thought it was all over. In March 1976, Susman got a call from the US attorney's office in Washington, which told him that it was going to convene a grand jury and get an indictment against the judge. Griffin Bell was US attorney at the time, and Judge Singleton knew him well.

Judge Singleton said, "I told Susman that I wanted to testify before the grand jury. He said, 'You can't do that.' And I said, 'Well, I'm going to do it.' We got a call from the United States attorney, and he said the grand jury was going to return an indictment, and that they just wanted me to know they would let me resign and make any statement I want to make. I was in my chambers. They were on the phone and Susman was with me. I said, 'Mark, tell them to kiss my ass.' Mark said, 'Oh, I can't do that.' I said, 'I don't give a damn. Just tell them to kiss my ass.' He did. The grand jury convened, and I insisted that I go before them. The word stressful is not even close to describing that day. I spent a whole day before them, and they called me back the next day."

He continues, "The US attorney's office kept telling me that the grand jury was going to return an eighty-one-count indictment that afternoon. It was a Friday, and after I finished testifying, I made all the arrangements to get out of town. I was sitting in my chair in chambers around 3:00 p.m. The marshall came in and said, 'Judge, did you know the grand jury left?' I said, 'No.' He said, 'No, they're gone.'"

The judge had to be under unbelievable stress and confusion about what was going on. He remembers, "Warren Burnett was a good friend of mine who was in chambers with me. He said we should go find out why they left. He wrote 'plea for information' on a piece of yellow paper and took it up to the United States attorney's office. One of the attorneys in the Justice Department came out and tore it up and said, "Look, we're leaving." They left. I have never heard another word about it. Susman found out that the grand jury voted eighteen to zero to not return the indictment and voted to have the foreman instruct the lawyers to go back to Washington and never come back to Houston again. I was just relieved. I didn't try to penalize anybody or do anything. In fact, I saw Griffin Bell later and told him I would like to find out who caused this indictment junk. He said, 'John, forget it. Don't go into it.' I never did."

When I asked the judge if that was what they call a bump in the road, he said, "Yes. The only one I ever had. In fact, before I went before the grand jury, I called a meeting of all my friends. We had a meeting at the courthouse—about thirty of them. I told them that they were trying to indict me and that I was going before the grand jury to testify. All the judges knew it, too. I had had a meeting with them, too."

Of all of the interesting stories the judge told me, the lesson for me with this one was on the importance of transparency and authenticity. He went before the grand jury against the advice of his lawyer, but because he wanted to tell the truth. He didn't know what the motivation was behind the investigation; he just wanted to tell his side of the story. Apparently, the grand jury found his testimony believable. He put his whole career and reputation on the line there. It was a big gamble. But it paid off. People are good about sensing what is real and what is fake. Clients appreciate authenticity and it is an important part of leadership. We don't have to be superheroes. Clients understand we are just people doing our best and sometimes we don't have all the answers. But, like Judge Singleton chose to do when faced with a big challenge, just telling the simple truth will most often win the day.

# Tell the Truth No Matter What the Cost

*John McKay*

John McKay, former US attorney for the Western District of Washington, was chosen as a director of the ABA Young Lawyers Division (YLD) by Judy Perry Martinez for her year as chair of the YLD, 1990–1991. We worked together as directors that year and focused on our service projects and learning leadership skills in the YLD. John says, "You know what I loved about young lawyers is that we all worked together on things that mattered, and everyone agreed they mattered, especially *pro bono* work—helping people who are powerless. In the Young Lawyers Division, we had a lot of fun, but what brought everybody together was that we worked on projects that actually helped people. We didn't say, hey, who's a Democrat and who's a Republican. It didn't make any difference."

My original interview was just after he had been fired as US attorney for the Western District of Washington. I had been to his office when he was the US attorney and knew that he loved his job and was very successful in that position. Although my lengthy interview had many highlights, when I asked John what his "LEAD line" was, he did not hesitate to say, "Tell the truth no matter what the cost." He has experienced several situations where this principle has guided his life and he has paid the price of being true to his conscience, but he is still one of the most influential and intelligent legal minds in America.

Foremost, John cherishes family. A self-proclaimed good Catholic boy, he says, "I'm one of twelve children, and that's pretty defining in a lot of ways. In our family, everything came down to a big round table in our house, where we ate dinner. My mother had a lazy Susan in the middle of the table. She didn't put the meat on it, because if you put the meat there it just didn't work. She would walk around and give us the meat. What happened around that table was my parents would lead a conversation about what was going on in the world. My earliest memories were of wanting to participate in the conversation. I'm the fifth of twelve, so I had four older siblings and seven younger siblings, so the way that conversation went, and what we talked about was probably the most important thing that happened to me and why I became a lawyer."

I asked him how that dinnertime conversation shaped his life, and he said, "Wanting to have a voice on what was happening. My parents would talk about what was going on in the world, what was going on in our immediate neighborhood, and what was going on in our family. It was more outward than inward. We talked more about what was happening out there and what our roles should be rather than who hit whom and our own internal squabbles. It was more like a classroom and a Socratic dialogue where we were called on, and our contribution related totally to our preparation and thoughtfulness. It was the pressure to participate that I remember feeling in the third grade."

John got into politics early and became the campaign manager for Joel Pritchard, the only Republican congressman in Washington State. They won. He describes the first time he went to Washington like this: "I was his campaign manager at twenty-one, and he won the election. I remember I was scared my first time going to D.C. I landed at National Airport and looked at the monuments and thought, 'Oh, my God. That's not the space needle down there. That's the Washington Monument. You ain't going to summer camp, boy. This is big time.'"

Even though he was scared, he started thinking, "So what?" He says, "I remember humming a tune to myself like, 'Let's see what happens next.' I developed a 'this isn't scary, this is fun' attitude. And what comes around the corner in life is how you react to it, how you handle yourself, how you treat others, and I learned that there. This wasn't just a class, this was real. People had real problems."

Several times in his career he has had a chance to tell the truth no matter the cost, and although it has not been easy, it is something that he passionately believes you must do to stay true to yourself. He says,

"When you know that doing the right thing is probably going to hurt you and maybe hurt some people around you, then you have to have a sense about yourself. I'll tell you about the sense I had when I got the phone call to tell me I was fired as US attorney. It's a sense that you've got to take some of the dirt, and it's going to hit you, and it's going to hurt, but the alternative is to look at yourself in the mirror and say, 'I didn't do the right thing when I should have done the right thing.'"

John had already been in that position a long time before with a Federal Bureau of Investigation (FBI) memo he wrote as a White House Fellow. He recalls, "That's hard because you know something bad is going to happen. I knew the minute I wrote the FBI memo as a White House Fellow I would have long-term consequences. When I wrote that memo, I knew that I was giving advice that they didn't want to hear. I knew it would be hard for them to hear it, but it was like an elephant in the room—someone had to say it. Actually, the more important thing to me was that I didn't want to do it, but it was the right thing, so I had to. I think it really has made a difference for me in my life." He continues, "There are a few other times in my life where I had to do the same thing. You've got to stand up, and you've got to say the thing, even when it's going to hurt you."

Years later, John paid the price for standing up when he was fired from his position as US attorney. He says, "One thing I regret about being fired is that I did a lot of work in law enforcement as the US attorney, the chief federal law enforcement official. There are a lot of stories from drug tunnels to human trafficking to amazing stuff, and I feel like I worked hard on those issues. I cared a lot about them, and my experience is defined by getting fired."

In fact, his office had just had a four-year performance review with rave reviews. The review is supposed to be done every three years, but ironically the same guy who ended up firing him called him up at the end of three years and said, "We know your office runs so well, we're going to put you off for a year." John says, "The Xerox paper was still warm. It had just happened. It was the most recently reviewed office out of the ninety-two offices, and the reviews included several best practices, which rarely get handed out. I knew that about my office, and now or shortly thereafter, I was being fired. I knew there would be a reason. It would have to come out. But I couldn't denounce it. I couldn't say this was wrong."

John gives this whole concept some deep thought before speaking and tells me, "I look back on it now and I can see why I got fired. Because I was never afraid to speak out in private, usually in private, but remember this is post-9/11. A lot of things happened where the Justice Department and the government were pushing the bounds of the Constitution to keep us safe. From Guantanamo, to wire-tapping, intelligence gathering, trying to prevent and disrupt terrorism, and the use of statutes."

"On at least two occasions, I spoke out in those meetings and raised questions about constitutionality of actions being undertaken by the government." He explains, "One time it was a meeting with the attorney general, and I thought to myself, 'This is unconstitutional. I don't think we can do this.' There were probably fifty US attorneys, the attorney general, and no staff in the room. And there was no discussion of the topic." He says, "I remember thinking to myself, if I stand up, it will look like I'm grandstanding, and I don't want to do that. Someone else would surely raise this issue because it was so obvious." John waited. He said, "The attorney general of the United States was running the meeting. I was sitting toward the front. I couldn't even look behind me to see if people were reacting. I waited, and I waited. I thought, this meeting is going to end, and fifty presidentially appointed US attorneys, with the presidentially appointed attorney general of the United States, have just discussed an issue of a very questionable constitutionality, and no one mentioned it."

Finally, McKay stood up and said, "Mr. Attorney General, I'm concerned about this aspect of this discussion. It makes me think that it is constitutionally dubious if someone is looking at this, and what's our responsibility?" I might as well have belched in the room. You should have seen the look on his face. I did not want to be the one to stand up and say it. But, one of us had to do it. So, I did it. I just didn't expect it was just going to be me. That was fairly early on in my tenure as US attorney, and I know I did the right thing from my standpoint. How could I have left that meeting saying, 'How come nobody said anything' when I was one of the people? I know for a fact that from that time on, I was seen as someone who was not going to go along with everything. That, more than anything else, is why I got fired. They knew I wasn't reliable to do whatever they said."

After the US attorney position ended, McKay became a professor at the Seattle University School of Law. He used his experiences to teach law students how to use their voices for justice. He says, "I tell my law students, you are all going to have a moment, and the moment is going to look like this. Someone's going to call you in, and they are going to tell you to do something that you know is wrong. And there are going to be stakes. You will see the stakes like this. You might lose your job. You might lose your house. Your family might not be in good shape for the next few weeks. You might not become partner. Or you know you should stay silent. You have to decide whether to say something, especially if they instruct you to do something that is going to be on you."

John is back in private practice in Seattle with the firm of Davis, Wright Tremaine LLP and is still as passionate about ethics and doing things right. His background taught him that and everything in his character leads him in the right direction. He says, "As lawyers, we can never let our guard down on the oversight we have in our profession and the high degree of fiduciary duty we have to our clients. We have so many opportunities each day to wiggle our way out of the truth, for our clients, for ourselves, but we must stand firm and do what we know is right."

In our increasingly conflicted world, where one person says something is true and another person calls it "fake news," it is hard to tell what is true and what is not. Be committed to focusing on being the best you can be and to always telling the truth no matter the cost. John McKay is a shining example of a man who, at every turn in his career, chose to tell the truth, no matter the cost. He withstood the storms and came out a better person.

# Think Anew

*John W. Clark, Jr.*

John Clark was born in Dallas in 1938, just as his father was rising through the corporate ranks of what was then known as Magnolia Petroleum Company—now part of ExxonMobil. He came from a conservative family and lived a conservative lifestyle. "I grew up pretty much with a silver spoon in my mouth, but I thought everyone had the same spoon in their mouths because in my neighborhood, I wasn't any different than anyone else." John coasted through life fairly easily until he hit college. "I never thought of my father as an alcoholic, nor was my mother an alcoholic, but there was a lot of alcohol consumed in my parents' home by themselves and their friends. Some of their friends I think probably were alcoholics." His first night at college, John blacked out.

"The next morning, I woke up and I thought I had found my best friend. I loved what alcohol had done to me. It made me feel different. A lot of the shyness I experienced in my earlier life was taken away, a lot of anxiety was diminished, and I loved it. It made me feel like I was a big guy, like I was an adult, and that I had come of age. I learned how to drink." After transferring to Southern Methodist University (SMU), John continued to drink. He was able to maintain close to a B average but was drinking almost every night with his roommates. Looking back, he says three of his five housemates were clearly alcoholics at that age. "At the time, it was just 'let the good times roll," and grades became relatively easy for me as long as I didn't try to be at the top of my class."

From there, John started law school, although he had little to no interest in being a lawyer. In fact, he hadn't even applied—his father drove down to SMU while John was touring a graduate school out of state, and SMU agreed to let John in based solely on his transcript, waiving the law school admission test, as long as John could start class the following Monday. On Monday, John was sitting in class with no idea what he had gotten himself into. By the time he graduated in 1963, he was in the top half of his class, he was married, and had a child on the way. He found a job at a small law firm where he primarily represented bars, restaurants, private clubs, and lobbied for optical interests. "All of that included a lot of alcohol consumption. Alcohol became a daily part of my life as a young lawyer."

John has always felt more comfortable creating business and bringing business into law firms than actually practicing law, a trait that carried him through his next job as a partner for five years. "I enjoyed doing that and it probably fit in also with my romance with alcohol."

John had a few different jobs, but his life was progressing as planned up through the mid-1980s. "Life was really good. I had two beautiful daughters and a loving wife, I had no mortgage on my home, and life was really good for me." Then, his firm shut down. He found a new job and asked only that they wouldn't complain if he didn't come back after lunch—he was used to having a liquid lunch and then staying out of the office for the rest of the day. "Somewhere I had the nagging sense that I had lost a certain amount of integrity." Throughout all this, he became involved in the Young Lawyers Division (YLD) of the ABA. From that "came the most defining moment of my life."

As part of the YLD, John was working with the General Practice Section (now the Solo, Small Firm & General Practice Division). In 1991, they had a meeting in Phoenix where they would select a nominee to become secretary of the section. John had agreed to submit his name. "I remember that weekend in Phoenix, I was being interviewed for this position, and I tried to put on a happy face. At the same time, I was getting phone calls from my wife saying that I had crossed the line, that she was going to get a divorce, and I was not welcome back in my own home. In the face of all that, I had to appear to be excited about the possibility of being secretary of the section. While my personal life was falling apart, I must have put on a pretty good appearance and presentation because I got selected to be the nominee of the nominating committee."

John flew home from to Phoenix to find his car in the front of the house, his clothes in the trunk, and papers on the way. He called a friend, Louise Raggio, a divorce attorney, and met her in her office the next morning. "I knew that I was not being a good father or a good husband, but I think, looking back on it, it was my view that as long as the bills got paid and they all got to go to camp and got to go to college and join sororities, that I was doing what I was supposed to do as a father."

His divorce attorney was the first one to suggest he may want to quit drinking. "That was the first time I recall anyone ever telling me that I might have a problem with alcohol." Looking back, he realizes there were other signs, other warnings, that his family probably had made loud and clear, but "I was so totally self-centered that I didn't pay attention to it." He saw one psychologist on Monday, another on Tuesday, and they both suggested he go off for treatment. However, John didn't want to be a "sober member of society." His only motivation was to save his marriage. Fortunately, that was enough. He went to a treatment center in Minnesota, and he says, "I loved every minute of it up there." He made connections with other lawyers who had found themselves in similar situations—one told him he had never lost a client because he was sober, which resonated with John. John was able to reconcile with his wife and moved home.

Shortly thereafter, John's wife found out she had an aggressive form of liver cancer. "She lived sixty days from the date it was discovered until the time she died. What I thought was important for so many years became very unimportant. I think to this day I have not totally balanced my life again. I still have very little interest in the practice of law and far more interest in trying to help people, whose lives have been damaged as a result of being an alcoholic, and there are a lot of those people around and a lot of them are lawyers."

Looking back, John is glad they were able to reconcile. He remarried four or five years after his wife died, and his new wife, Barbara, is now a lawyer and practices with him as partner in his law practice. He says, "I spend a lot of time working through the state bar, through the ABA trying to help other people find the kind of happiness in life and the kind of serenity and peace that I have found being a sober member of society now. "When you stretch a rubber band, it stretches so far, and then it breaks, and it pops. Or you bend a stick and it breaks. That is what happened to me. Once that rubber band broke and once the stick cracked, I was able to really look at my life far more honestly than I had ever been willing to before."

To this day, he continues to try to do the best in whatever he's doing and tries not to be trapped in old thinking. It is a joy to have him participating in the GPSolo Division as an elder and the work he does to share his story is truly admirable. He admonishes lawyers to be willing to think anew: new ideas, new plans, new results.

# Be the Solution

*Pamela Fagan Hutchins*

Pamela was born to parents who were high school sweethearts. They ran away, eloped and put themselves on a path of hard work and family. She says, "For better or worse, they had to embrace it because of their choices." At her father's medical school graduation when she was a toddler, she had her first memory of her father's philosophy of "take the bull by the horns," and "don't ever be scared to jump off those cliffs." She says, "My mom is my best friend; my dad is my inspiration. It's really wonderful to have that."

From a very early age, like many women, Pamela's identity was based almost entirely on how those around her viewed her. She remembers being four years old and being told how beautiful she was. She was born with a beauty mark that she never wanted removed because it was a reminder—she was kissed by beauty. "Growing up believing that I was beautiful, which at one point is an external and shallow belief, does have an impact on who you are as you grow up."

Pamela is a lawyer and a prolific fiction writer. In third grade she had a defining moment when her third-grade teacher told her parents that someday she would be a famous novelist. She said, "I don't like to write; I like to read." But the notion stayed with her. Growing up, Pamela was the cheerleader, the homecoming queen, the blonde-haired, blue-eyed Barbie doll girl. But she was still "the brainy one."

By the time she graduated high school, Pamela was being told she could "argue anyone blue in the face, that she was a dissenter, and a justice-minded person." She says, "I was primed to think I was going to go to law school, and I didn't need this writing stuff." She made a near perfect score on her SAT, attended Texas A&M University, and then continued on to law school.

"For me, some of my defining moments as a woman and as a lawyer came because of the repetition of the idea in society that 'you are beautiful, and you should define yourself by what men think of you.'" In other words, she needed to be stupid to be approachable. Those images placed on her by other people led to incredible self-esteem issues. Pamela developed depression, she became bulimic, and she started drinking too much.

Being a young woman lawyer in the early 1990s was no easy task. Pamela joined a firm of about thirty lawyers and was only the third woman to ever work there. "It was a big tax firm and I had a male mentor attorney. She says, "I got assigned to somebody who is supposed to teach you the ropes. He's married; he's got kids." While Pamela was focused solely on her career, her mentor's wife had other things on her mind. They met at a company party and bumped into each other in the restroom. "She told me that I better keep my 'Barbie doll self' away from her husband." Pamela hadn't done a single thing other than be herself. She says, "At the same time the men are scared of you and don't look past your looks to see that you can kick their rears."

It wasn't easy for women in those days, but Pamela never shies away from a problem—she takes pride in being a problem-solver. "Find the place where there is a positive outcome possible and focus all your positive energy on making that happen. Identify the problem and be the solution." Instead of succumbing to the rampant sexism in the legal profession, Pamela kept moving.

She went on to work for West, where for a while she enjoyed great success. "Then this partner puts his hand on my leg and invites me to come with him to the horse races that next weekend while his wife was out of town and says I should stay at their place. I was devastated because at that moment you realize that it may not be because you're smart after all. Everybody may have been right, and it may be because of your bra size, the color of your hair, the shape of your eyes, or whatever it is, because they are not listening to you; they are not seeing you; they are not seeing what's inside."

Again, Pamela recognized the problem, recognized that she was not the problem, and then put her mind to solving it. "I went into a partnership with a friend of mine who was practicing employment law and we started a company called Employment Practices Solutions, and I took my crystallizing experiences with my feelings about those experiences with me."

Finally, Pamela felt that she had balance between the beauty that people saw her as and the brains she knew she was. "But it was because of the example my father instilled in me, by all these moments growing up as a woman, caught between that Encyclopedia Fagan and Barbie doll image where I wanted to be both. I didn't want just one to define me; I wanted to be the whole me. I wanted there to be balance. I learned that it's okay to be a force of nature—sometimes the tornado or the hurricane—because you're not there just to be a pretty, pleasing face. You can be all the stuff that makes all the colors of your rainbows. You're not a bitch, you're not a ball breaker, you're not an arm trophy, you're not just supposed to be quiet and sweet and smile. You can go in and be strong and assertive and smart and beautiful if you want to be, or you can look your worst that day and you're still awesome. You can be you."

As she moved throughout her career, Pamela started using how others saw her, once a constricting vice, and started working with it. She truly became a part of her own success by being part of her own solution.

But it's never just been a one and done for Pamela—she's continued to fight for herself and her future. She withstood an unhappy marriage and got divorced. Like many who divorce, she agonized over worrying about how her parents might see it as a failure, how they might think that she was no longer the perfect daughter upholding the perfect ideals they had placed on her. But she did it for herself and she did it to solve a problem.

In 2003, she quit drinking after one of her third-grade son's teachers approached her and said, "Clark told me he is worried about you." Pamela was stunned. "My third-grade child should not have to tell anybody that." She immediately went to her boss, then went to a spa in St. Lucia where she got blackout drunk and woke up still in her clothes in the bathtub. That was the last time she ever drank. "That was a big defining moment for me—admitting I had a problem with alcohol. I have a problem with surrounding myself with the wrong people because of alcohol. Now I've gotten rid of both."

Pamela is happily remarried to Eric Hutchins and living a sober life. In 2018 she became a *USA Today* bestseller and Silver Falchion Best

Mystery winner. Her husband took his last drink on their first date. "We pretty much went from first date to we're going to spend the rest of our lives together." From day one, they were all in. She sees her progression throughout life as an "evolution in putting things in order," and from there the right things came to be. She became a devoted mother and started working out of her house to raise her kids. Through the pains of child rearing and working from home, her husband still constantly tells her, "You're still an ass-kicking goddess of the St. Croix Rainforest that you believed yourself to be." Overcoming people pleasing, bulimia, alcoholism, and beauty perfection wasn't easy but it sure provides fuel for the award-winning novels that keep getting written at light speed.

# Use Your Past to Shape Your Future

*Tabitha Charlton*

---

Tabitha is a Texas girl, born to a fifteen-year-old mother. She learned resilience at a young age. Tabitha's parents got divorced when she was seven, the same age her mom was when her own mother abandoned her and her little brother. They were left with their loving, albeit alcoholic, father who, in turn, left them to be raised by his sister and her husband, who were poor farmers with three young kids of their own, including a disabled son.

Tabitha says, "My home life in my early childhood was good; I was an only child for four years and I was the center of my mother's world. When my parents married, my dad's parents took in my mom as one of their own and basically raised us both . . . but things changed when I was four or five. Unbeknownst to my parents, a neighbor started molesting me and I did not know to report it and by the time I did, I was too afraid of being punished." Tabitha's father wasn't home much and her mother, herself still a teenager, naively assumed Tabitha's change in behavior was due to the birth of her little sister, which ultimately formed the first breaks in Tabitha's strong bond with her mother. Her mother's remarriage was the final break.

"My mom remarried and everything changed." Tabitha's stepfather moved them away from her father's family and his parents, who were the primary stability in her life. "He changed all the rules . . . I was suddenly punished for things that had been okay all my life. My grandma always painted our nails when we were with her, but that was no longer allowed in his house. Well, we came home from grandma's house one Sunday night and I got in trouble because my grandma painted my nails red. . . . So, it didn't take long for things to go bad." Tabitha's step-dad's form of discipline—using belts and whips—may have been acceptable when he was being raised, but was no longer when he was raising kids.

In sixth grade, Tabitha reported all of the abuse to her teacher and CPS was called. Though she was never placed in foster care, Tabitha spent the next four years shuffling among family members.

Not even school offered a reprieve for Tabitha. "I was going through a lot at home. I felt unwanted, unloved, insignificant. I had horrible self-esteem and I believed I wasn't worthy of anyone's love, so that made me awkward and I was picked on a lot."

When she turned to her biological father to save her, he was more interested in being a bachelor than a father to a fifteen-year-old girl. "I went to live with my dad my freshman year in high school, but dad wasn't capable of supervising me and he had a bad temper. I was there for nine months when CPS removed me from his home. There were no foster homes available or willing to take me so, CPS gave me a choice—I could go to a girls' home or return to my mother. I had not spoken to my mom in months and, honestly, I wanted nothing to do with her or my stepfather, but I agreed to meet her with my case worker. . . ."

Tabitha ultimately chose to stay with her mom after her hearing her mom's own story. "My mom cried a lot that day. She begged me to move back in with her, assuring my stepfather was working out of town and would not interact with me, but I was unconvinced until she told about the time she lived in an orphanage and how badly she did not want that to happen to me." Tabitha finished high school living with her mom and, at eighteen, she was out the door and gone.

Tabitha used her pain and anger to fuel her own success. She is the first person in her family to graduate high school. Tabitha worked her way through college, often working two to three jobs to make ends meet and pay for school. She did the same to put herself through law school, and when that wasn't enough, she couch-surfed, lived in her car, and took out extensive student loans. The one thing she never did was give up.

Tabitha credits her childhood with driving her will to succeed. Her refusal to quit, even in the face of the toughest adversity, led her to becoming a lawyer. She saw how the Texas Department of Family

Protective Services got involved in her life time and time again and nothing got better. While she was planning her career, Tabitha considered all the different possibilities in how to help children with upbringings similar to hers. "I wanted to do family law. I know what's going on from both angles. That was my reason for going to law school." However, things didn't get easier for her as a family lawyer.

Tabitha's driving force was tested in her very first case involving a single mom who had three children out of wedlock by the same man. The mother had evicted the father from her home, but wanted to establish visitation, custody, and child support. She was assured "it should be a pretty easy case, no big deal." Tabitha met her client and was inspired by her story, but things quickly became difficult once she began working on the case. "The father started filing frivolous motions and the harassment started. He would call me every fifteen minutes and harass me." Then he began making death threats—against the mom, Tabitha, the judge, and anyone who crossed his path. He even killed the mom's cat. Ultimately, the mom won the case.

But that was not the end. He decided to kill her. He bought a crow bar. She says, "On Christmas Eve in 2009, he set the house on fire. When she answered the door, he killed her right there by the Christmas tree, in front of the kids. He is now in prison for life, without the possibility of parole. The kids escaped and were later adopted by her best friend."

The case shaped Tabitha and made her into the lawyer and professional she is today. "I fought hard for my client because I felt like this case came to me for a reason. I felt like nobody could fight for her as hard as I would. Half the time, I didn't even know what the heck I needed to do next because there was no precedent for dealing with this level of insanity and harassment by a *pro se* opposing client. I learned along the way." To this day, she continues to fight for children in any and every way possible.

After almost seven years at Norton Rose Fulbright (formerly Fulbright & Jaworski), Tabitha left to start a nonprofit organization, Kidsave Texas, that works to find families for older kids in foster care. Tabitha's passion for Kidsave pours out of her when she talks about it. "When we launch our Weekend Miracles program in Houston later this year, we will be the only program in the state singularly focused on finding loving, stable, permanent families for older kids and teens stuck in the cycle of foster care. We have a real problem of capacity in our foster care system and the hardest demographic to place is teen girls, just like me . . . a lot of these kids get stuck in a cycle of residential treatment centers, where they are raised by shift workers instead of loving families. Kidsave's Weekend Miracles program matches these youth with host families who agree to in-person visits with them at least twice a month and, over time, become their advocates, mentors, and, in many cases, their guardians and adoptive families."

Despite her tough background and rocky beginning, Tabitha has shaped a life she is proud of. She is now director of Kidsave Texas, and serves as chief operating officer for Boudreaux, Hunter & Associates, goals anyone who knew of her background, but didn't know her, might have thought she would never achieve. She exemplifies the lead line of "Use your past to shape your future."

# Practice Gratitude Daily

*Hon. John Kralik*

---

At a young age, someone suggested to John he should be a writer. He had a father who was an extremely hard worker and who had enormously high expectations of his children. John knew it wasn't for him—he wanted to be useful, helpful, and do meaningful work, and he didn't see writing as a way to accomplish that. "I tried law school and I think that was a defining moment when I got back my grade and I realized I was good at it, which surprised me. I decided to hang with it."

John was driven, hardworking, and wouldn't let anything stand in his way of being made partner in a Wall Street firm—unfortunately, not even his marriage. "Once you start as an associate in a big firm you get this overwhelming desire that you are not going to be one of the washouts. You are going to work hard to make partner. I think that I should have realized that the job was one that made it difficult to be married. I just wasn't available enough. And after working so many long hours, there was nothing left emotionally to share with a partner. I think anybody who has worked at one of the big law firms, I'm sure it's the same now as it was then, maybe even more so, knows that the pressure to bill hours is great. To bill 2,700 to 2,800 real valuable good hours in a year, I mean there really isn't much left of you after that."

When he was ready to marry for the second time, he changed jobs to reopen his emotional availability. He says, "I took an in-house job with an oil company where I worked for seven years, and I was more available both in my marriage and my personal life. When I was about forty-five, I found the company was being sold and it was an opportunity where if I took the severance package, I would have enough money to start my own firm. I always wanted to practice law my way. Some people thought I should see a psychologist for doing such a bold thing. We had no business at all."

He opened his own practice and in his best-selling book, *365 Thank You's: The Year a Simple Act of Daily Gratitude Changed My Life,* he writes about the struggles along the way with such honesty and freshness. I highly recommend the book to you. When I read it, I was so impressed that finally someone told the truth about the law. We walk around with these big smiles and post all of our successes on Facebook, but no one sees us in the middle of the night worrying about payroll and when that client is going to pay their bill. We have such an image of strength to portray that showing what is underneath when your world is falling apart is almost verboten.

John isn't afraid to be vulnerable. He laid it all out there and the response he got was overwhelming. I reached out to him after reading the book and we became friends in the process. He says, "After ignoring the suggestions that I might be nuts, I did it, and my book portrays a very bad and discouraging year, but I had some good years and, generally, was making it. We built up to seven or eight people, so we had started something from scratch. It was successful."

He says, "I wrote what I call a statement of ideals." John laid out on paper a survey of his law firm, his ideals and morals, and essentially created a mission statement of his work. He was determined to maintain the ability to persuade those around him to do the right thing and say no to clients that would steer them in the wrong direction. He created a workplace that was more than just a workplace; it was like a family. John says, "There is a part in the book where I note how I came to that realization, but yes, those people are like family members. That's what I wanted. That doesn't always get you the right amount of money. It sometimes requires enormous extra effort and I think, sadly, that extra effort and the fact that I wanted to do such an unusual, time-consuming, overwhelming thing of starting my own law firm at age forty-five, that ended up costing me a second marriage. That was a heavy price to pay."

Eventually though, practicing law wore John down. "I always had this feeling that I wasn't quite correctly cast as a lawyer. That became a stronger and stronger feeling, and it motivated me to apply to be a judge. Throughout my career many people who knew me and talked about my feelings about the law and my job, would tell me you really need to be a judge because you'll be more comfortable, and your talents can be used. While I was miscast, I had spent thirty years soaking up knowledge of the law and was actually pretty good at it."

John found his niche in being a judge. He recalls his father who was very opinionated about his children and hard work and says, "I was trying to prove that although I wasn't going to be a surgeon like him, I would be very good at what I did. I think as he got older, he got more generous and I believe he was very impressed by the fact that I'm a judge."

He went through the arduous process that people go through to become a judge in California. He had tried three years earlier and was convinced he would not be accepted. I had the awesome experience of going to his chambers and seeing him in action. He says, "I think being a judge is a wonderful job if you can get it. I think that's why everyone wants it. I think you can describe a job like that to anyone coming out of college saying this is the job I'm going to have for you to do, to figure out some difficult and sometimes interesting situations, to figure out what the law is, and to apply it in a fair manner and to be respectful and honest in doing it," he says with a smile. He continues, "It's a public service as well in that a lot of the cases in truth wouldn't be described as interesting and they are repetitive, but you're doing a public service, so there is also that gift."

Being a judge allowed him time to finish his book. He learned through his time as a lawyer and the beginning of his career as a judge that "honest writing is more useful." John has always valued honesty, even when it was difficult to be so. "It had been a difficult thing to decide to be honest. I will say I had a great deal of fear about writing about my life at the time because you see so many good people completely trashed in our society and really vicious things written about quite nice people in quite nice books. But what I got in return was really lovely, thankful emails filled with love and gratitude and people who say they are inspired by me. As I read the difficulties that they were going through, I feel inspired by them because there are many people going through worse difficulties than me."

John still practices gratitude daily. "I have a chance every day really to make a positive difference and to be a good judge. It's a big job in the sense that it's an important and big responsibility and to use that right. I'm sure I'll make mistakes and not get everything right, but I strive to do the best I possibly can." He set out early in life wanting to do something that was "gainful and that was good for the world." John has more than succeeded in meeting his goal and he has helped so many others along the way too with his refreshing authenticity and skill as a writer.

# Know Thyself and Always Have a Team

*Nina L. Kaufman*

Nina always knew she wanted to be a lawyer. She grew up in a suburb of New York City that was known for its exceptional public schools and high college placements. She grew up never wanting for anything and was "amply provided for." It was never a question for Nina whether she would go to college. "By the time I was twelve or thirteen, I had already decided that I would go to law school."

Like many of the lawyers in this book, one of the shaping factors in Nina's decision was seeing *To Kill a Mockingbird* at an impressionable age. "I think what stuck with me was a lot of the images of lawyers at that time—Atticus Finch; Perry Mason. I was interested in people who had an intrepid spirit who really wanted to get to the truth, who wanted to get the justice, and particularly in the case of Atticus Finch. He was a wise, trusted counselor in a community fraught with a lot of problems, and he was one of the few voices of reason. He was a great man of integrity."

Once Nina started law school, she realized the task she had just taken on. "My experience of law school initially was like going ninety miles per hour into a brick wall. I had to think in a different way for whatever reason. I couldn't pick it up quite as easily as I could all my college subjects." At the same time, during her first semester, she was trying to finish up her master's dissertation and her grandfather passed away. It was a really challenging time. Although she got used to the pace and subject matter of law school, and ultimately found success, she told me "that semester sort of shaped the beginning of my career."

Another more shining moment of law school was Nina's success on Boston University's moot court team. She had no coach, her team had little experience, and Nina loved her position as the swing speaker. Her passion made up for what they lacked. They ultimately made it to the winner's dinner at the Union League Club in Chicago. "We were the little orphan team that wasn't expected to do anything. The teams that did not win broke down and cried. To some extent I think being really relaxed about our experience because we didn't think we would win may have made us exude a confidence and ability that made us come across very favorably. That's been a lesson I have learned over and over again since then, but it is a big highlight of my life."

That experience taught Nina to rely on herself as opposed to "the experts, because the experts were cautioning us not to get our hopes up too much."

From there, Nina thought she would go into litigation after graduation, but over the next few years discovered she didn't have the same passion for it. "I thought for a long time that I had in some way failed; that I had chickened out. I just didn't have the stomach for it. Maybe on some level that is what it was, but I realized that litigation is not what I wanted to do; I loved appellate practice." But to get to that, Nina had to go through a lot first.

First, she set out on her own for several reasons. She noticed attorneys were not being trained from within to get more specialized skills. And, the firms where she worked were not making women partners. She heard the story of a woman who had been working in big law doing antitrust litigation, who was making six figures a year, and everything was golden—then the case ended. "When the case ended, she got fired. For ten years, she had been working on this teeny, little piece of antitrust litigation, she was an associate in the double digits, so she's been out for more than ten years, all she knows is this very narrow area of law, and she couldn't get a job for love or money."

Nina saw this woman that had bought into the story of working hard in a law firm to achieve recognition and compensation, and then she saw that floor fall out from under her. Nina knew she couldn't, wouldn't let the same thing happen to her. She started asking herself, "How am I going to have more control over my destiny? Because I did not want somebody fifteen years in the future saying, 'Thanks very much, Ms. Kaufman, but we just don't need you. Gather your things and don't let the door hit you on the way out.'"

Nina found a mentor in law school, and they went to into business together for a time. "That's where I learned some hard lessons about what it means to go into business with friends. In retrospect, there were a lot of ways I comported myself in business because I was with a friend that I would not necessarily have done had it been an arm's length business transaction." To those considering it, she advises having a third-party advisor or strategic consultant to oversee discussions. She advises against giving too much of yourself away.

The problems started early on, when Nina realized her personal development had surpassed those of the business. Then, she got married and her priorities, by necessity, had to change. She wanted to "create a business that I could leverage so I had more free time to start a family and travel and do the other things that I enjoy doing, like public speaking." Finally, after many attempts, Nina had to bite the bullet and tell her partner she wasn't in it anymore. "Once he got wind of 'Oh she's going to have her own practice. She just doesn't want to do it with me,' he took it very personal and things really deteriorated from there."

Nina told me the first warning sign was when she and her partner stopped communicating. They fell into their different silos of work and stopped speaking to each other. In retrospect, Nina would have liked to schedule once-a-month strategy sessions supplemented with weekly check-ins. "You have to set some time where you are both clear on what's going to unfold."

Even after navigating through a nasty business divorce, Nina had to work hard to accomplish what she wanted. For a while, her biggest wall was even visualizing what it meant to have a solo practice, and the type of success she wanted to create. To achieve even that, she looked back to Socrates. "To really know thyself and appreciate who you are, what your genuine talents are, and what your real desires for your life are. Law is so much of a status-oriented profession. It's difficult to step back from that and say you're going to take a different path, and that path is just as valid." She now also knows that her best lessons won't come from a book or a masterclass—they will come from her own mistakes. Serving others and helping them to find their true selves is her passion.

# Prioritize Human Connection

*Wilson Adam Schooley*

Wil's life now exemplifies authenticity, but it was a developed skill. It did not come naturally or without effort. Wil was born in 1957, at a tumultuous time in an exciting place: Berkeley, California. One of his brothers participated in the Freedom Rides with Dr. Martin Luther King in Alabama and Mississippi. He was in the first class of voluntary integration in the country where they bussed the students down to the black neighborhood and the white schools were integrated too. When there were riots at the University of California while he was in grammar school, he would be released early because of tear gas alerts and would go up Telegraph Avenue to watch the Free Speech Movement unfold.

He says, "All that was very dramatic and shaped my perspective on a lot of things that were to come. My heroes at the time were people like my brothers, Dr. King, and Malcolm X, and other people who were making change in a sensational way."

From an early age the plight of those who were affected by injustice caught his imagination. "When you see people who are profoundly affected by injustice, you have a drive to work for justice. I think it was the political and social environment that led me in the direction of practicing law because I was very interested in civil rights and human rights. When I got to a point in college where I had to decide what I wanted to do, that was the background that guided me in the direction of law school." One of his professors suggested he go to a top law school in the South, an area still afflicted by social injustice.

The thing I find most fascinating about Wil is the fact that he was a shy child with a tendency to keep an emotional distance from others. He says, "I was so shy, almost pathologically shy as a kid. My parents were middle-western, very taciturn, very nondemonstrative, folks—good folks. I was extremely shy—a very unlikely person to be an attorney." Wil was almost held back in first or second grade because he never spoke. One of his teachers came to him and told him, "You are incredibly smart, but you never talk. You won't even answer when I ask you a direct question." She helped encourage him and brought him out of his shell enough to do well in school. He says, "It was still something that plagued me so that even during college and law school, if I had a public presentation to make, I would cut class. I just wouldn't go."

Wil thinks it was partly genetic because his father was a very introspective writer and noncommunicative. He has a British Scandinavian Midwestern background, which lends itself to stoicism, but they were also Depression-era folks. He says, "It's also part of the way that I am emotionally, physiologically. I've always been very emotional, and I think that tends to make you self-protective because if you put yourself out there, your emotions are at risk, so you tend to just shut down and close the doors. All those things together contributed to making me like I was. I could barely talk to myself."

By the time he was in law school he was forced to break out of it somewhat because of the structure of the classes and getting called on during class. He went to law school because of his passion for justice and civil rights. He did not know that he was going to have to be called upon in class. He tried to avoid it at all costs. He would get sick and not show up when he had a presentation.

To pursue his dream of helping others conquer injustice, he had to overcome his fear of public speaking. When he got into practice he became a transactional lawyer, which he hated. His dreams of doing civil rights began to drift away. His breakthrough came when his law firm, a great firm, hired an actress and director to coach all of the lawyers on presentation skills. He went through the drills with the coach. He says, "She did these horrifying exercises. One, we had to have a partner and stand a foot away from each other and look directly into their eyes for five minutes without speaking. I was paired up with a senior tax law partner. He was the scariest man in the world. Everyone was scared of him. I had to look in the man's eyes for five minutes straight. It was incredibly hard. All that self-protection is pretty tough to maintain. It was horrifying."

At the end, the actress pulled him aside and told him she was casting a play and told him that she thought he would be wonderful in it and would he do it for her? Wil was petrified but he did it. It was a comedy improv show where you not only had to get up in front of people, but you didn't have a script. It went well, and someone saw him, and he got cast in something else. He got an agent who asked him to do television and film. Wil became more and more comfortable as time went on and became a litigator. He developed a dual career with the support of his family and his firm.

In the 1990s he reached a fork in the road. His law firm had dissolved after seventy years and he was recruited to another firm. But the work–life balance was hard to maintain at that firm. He decided his choices were to go to another firm and try to make it work, or he could do what he originally went into the law to do, which was fight for the rights of people who are underprivileged. He resigned his partnership and took up indigent criminal defense on appeal. He got on the panel where you get assigned the cases, which was not an easy feat. He began getting paid about one-fifth of what he made in private practice. It was a difficult decision and it was complicated by the fact that he had a health issue at the time, extreme cardiac arrhythmia and tachycardia. Fortunately, he had a good strong heart and they did a procedure called ablation, and it was made better.

In addition to criminal appellate defense and acting, Wil teaches advocacy. He says, "Law school was about learning in two dimensions—reading and writing. Then you're suddenly expected, like I was, to stand up in three-dimensions and communicate with real people—jurors—about real things. For a long time, law school didn't teach students that. They taught lawyers how to think like a lawyer and that doesn't go over very well with jurors. Jurors want the emotion; they want to feel like you feel in a movie or in a play; they want to feel the emotion. People are hopelessly willing to suspend disbelief in order to become emotionally involved in something. What I teach my law students is how to be themselves. Because what you've lost in being so wrapped up in the law, is yourself. You've lost your heart; you've lost your ability to communicate to other human beings in a human way. What I teach allows the students to be human in front of people; to talk like humans; to make eye contact with their juries and relay to them emotionally legal concepts and truths but do it in a human emotional way that conveys the real impact behind what's happening instead of legalism."

The highlight of his acting career is when he was cast to play Atticus Finch in *To Kill a Mockingbird*. He says, "I did *To Kill a Mockingbird*, which is maybe the dream role for a lawyer who is an actor, at the Onstage Playhouse in San Diego and it was very well received. We sold out every night and everybody loved it. People, over and over, would come up to me with tears coming down their faces saying, 'I was so moved. This is my favorite book/movie that I've ever read/seen, and you brought it so much to life. You were Atticus. I've never felt anything like that. You moved me so much.' That's the kind of thing—that human connection—is what we all live for." He has had numerous occasions to play the role again and it is a great thing for him and his audiences.

Wil says, "When you see people who are dramatically affected by injustice, you have a drive to work for justice." Through many trials and tribulations, he is living his dream of being an actor, law professor, and champion of the downtrodden. It is no wonder that Wil has served as chair of the American Bar Association Section of Civil Rights and Social Justice. Working tirelessly and often under the radar, he is now living the dreams he envisioned as a child and works to make justice appear where injustice resides.

# You've Got to Be in It to Win It

*Robert J. Grey, Jr.*

Robert is the product of a military father and an educator mother. His father was stationed in Europe when he was a young child and that expanded his worldview. When he returned to the States, he couldn't speak English, only French. He returned to a segregated Richmond, Virginia. Oliver W. Hill, of *Brown v. Board of Education* fame and a close friend of Supreme Court Justice Thurgood Marshall, was a neighbor and became a good friend and mentor. Buck Wilder, who was the first African American governor elected in the country, lived close.

Robert remembers, "We lived in a duplex in what I guess would be some middle-class part of town and I went to public schools. Shortly after, we moved into a house of our own instead of sharing a house with another family. Richmond was segregated; the county was segregated; everything was segregated. I did not come into contact with people other than those of my own race. Personally, I did not feel the discomfort of segregation as I was growing up."

During that time, segregation was not apparent to the kids and in Robert's close-knit community, everybody took care of each other. There were a lot of kids on his block and the parents were comprised of school teachers to bricklayers, to restaurant owners, photographers, and even the president of the teachers' association. Robert says, "It was a mix of everybody and no one thought they were more important than anybody else. I lived near Battery Park. There were tennis courts, basketball courts, and I played there and interacted with the kids in my neighborhood."

Robert was adventurous and like any teenager he liked to "test the outer limits of things." He says, "Instead of paying to go to the baseball game, it was more fun hopping the fence. I hopped the fence one time and got my pants caught in the barbed wire. It was exciting to have the security people running after me. We got to the seats and I felt wet. I thought it was maybe a spilled drink on my seat. But the wetness was my blood. I caught my thigh when I jumped over that fence. Explaining that one when I got home was interesting to say the least. But those were the things that kids did and that's about as brazen as I got challenging the law."

When Buck Wilder ran for the senate in the early 1970s, no other African American had been elected to the senate of Virginia since reconstruction. Robert remembers, "That was a big deal and he ran a campaign that nobody in their wildest imagination thought he would win, but he did. That changed things socially. I can remember that for the first time, I actually felt I could do something different and that I could be part of the larger community the same way that the majority community had been running itself. It was an eye-opener, it was a door-opener, and it was something that jolted me to say, 'You know what? You can think larger than you're thinking about things.'"

His activism and devotion to his community has roots in his childhood and everything he experienced. His parents instilled community service in him at an early age. He says, "If there is any one thing that I saw that was crystal clear to me, it was that you have a responsibility to participate. You can't just sit on your hands and watch and let other people do it."

During the civil rights movement, Virginia engaged in something called "massive resistance." Massive resistance was the thought that "We'll close the schools before we integrate them." Robert says, "If the federal court said as a result of *Brown v. The Board of Education*, you must integrate the schools, then they closed the schools. They closed a number of schools in the state protesting and contesting the *Brown* dispute. It lasted long enough, but through the efforts of Oliver Hill and people like Lewis Powell, who was chairman of the Richmond School Board, they eventually got the governor to stop that nonsense. It was eventually abandoned."

Massive resistance did create a much more active political community in the black community after that. The Crusade for Voters came out of this movement and it is the oldest black political organization in Richmond. Robert's mother was one of the early members of Crusade for Voters. He remembers how his mother told him he had to put slips of paper in people's doors to ask them to vote. In elementary school, he ran around sticking notices in people's doors to get them out to vote.

Another big influence on Robert in the early years was the fact that his maternal grandmother lived with him all of his life. He says, "That's what you did back then. Your grandparents lived with you if that was the best option. One of the shows that she let me watch with her was *Perry Mason*. I liked him and the fact that he never lost. I think the influences of Oliver Hill, Doug Wilder, and Perry Mason made me consider law school. He says, "But the thing that pushed me over the top about law as a career was the fact that it allows for a degree of independence. You could be your own boss and practice law and provide a service. That was a big motivator for me."

Like so many lawyers of a certain generation, Robert worked during high school, college, and in law school. In high school he worked at the grocery store and became a unionized cashier. He credits that job with teaching him some of the diplomacy skills he uses today. He says, "I learned how to decide difficult issues, how to weigh the pros and cons of making a critical decision, and how to exercise judgment." In college, he worked at an office supply store.

Robert got slowed down a little bit by the fact that he got drafted to Vietnam while he was in college. His number was fifty-two. His father was in the military so there was no getting out of it. He went to get his physical and got rejected on the basis of medical reasons because he is highly allergic to eggs. The military then was using a lot of powdered eggs in the diet, so it was a no-brainer. The Army doctor looked at him and said, "Son, we'd kill you before they would." He sent him home.

Robert went straight back to school. It was a tumultuous time as the community was integrating and things were changing. He felt like the community was coming a long way but that it still had a long way to go. He remembers going to a YMCA camp when he was growing up and he was the only black kid at the camp. People sometimes made fun of him, but most of the people were nice. He says, "You had to be mindful of the fact that some people don't like you just because you're black. It was a disappointment to me, but it didn't stop me from doing anything."

Robert let me know that there are still some places that are very segregated. He joined an all-white golf club because he liked the club and has had no funny looks or unkind words. He says, "We are still breaking barriers, we're still on this path of creating a different society that is inclusive today. The way to do it is to get a little bit beyond this idea of fear and being uncomfortable. The only way you can do that is to give yourself permission to extend your boundaries a little bit. Personal and professional boundaries. If you do that you tend to take more risks. If you take more risks, there is a higher chance of reward. There will be some disappointments for sure, but there is a higher likelihood of reward and of accomplishing what we are trying to accomplish, which is a more inclusive society. But you've got to give yourself permission, and then you've got to go do it. You have to take some risks."

Robert is a self-proclaimed risk taker. He says, "That has been one of the most fundamental principles of my existence. I tried to get a job with a major law firm—couldn't. I started my own law firm. I couldn't make enough money to support myself, so I taught school at my alma mater and supported myself to start my practice. I was working two jobs. But you take a risk—like opening my own office and supporting myself by teaching—and it pays off. Four years later, I got invited by the governor to give up my practice and become a member of the Alcohol and Beverage Control Board. That was a risk because I had developed a pretty good real estate practice and court-appointed criminal work. I had a good pipeline working where I was learning, growing, and teaching. It was fun. I was the happiest then professionally that I have ever been.

Two things about the job at the Alcohol and Beverage Control Board are that he was the first African American to be appointed to the commission and he was the youngest to ever serve. At thirty-four, not only did he have to interact with people who had been running a specialized industry, but he had to deal with people who were much his senior. He dealt with it by telling them he needed their help. He said, "I don't know this, but you do. I want to be successful and I want you to help me be successful. I want you to teach me what I don't know." He says, "And I listened. I had to make some important decisions along the way, but I never did them without good counsel and advice, and I never made a critical decision without having all the facts, giving people their say, and making sure that I covered all the bases that needed to be covered so that I could make a fair, advised decision."

Like his good friend, Dennis Archer, Robert has had the honor of being the first of many things in his life. He says, "It reminds you that we have come a long way and that we have a long way to go." In the 1980s he was president of the Richmond Crusade for Voters. He became the second African American president of the American Bar Association.

One of the biggest risks he has taken in his career is what spawned his LEAD line: You've got to be in it to win it. He says, "When I ran for mayor of Richmond, I didn't have any name recognition and I started really late and had everything to lose. And I lost." When pondering what he learned from that experience, after all of his many and varied successes, he says, "It's okay to lose a big thing because you have to pick yourself up off the ground and get on with it. I had not taken that kind of fall. You just have to pick yourself up. It's a crushing defeat to lose. Especially with people who think you should win. One thing I did learn is that 'you have to be in it to win it.' And that means you've got to have a burning desire to win. Your appetite has to be insatiable. I did not go out and seek anybody's permission or encouragement to run. But, my heart was not in it. What doesn't kill you makes you stronger. That's the truth. I cannot walk into a grocery store, or drug store, or airport, or something, each month without somebody saying, 'I voted for you.'"

Robert learned a great lesson from that at a crucial stage in his life and he is still taking risks, but he is doing things he wants to do rather than what others want him to do. He served as the executive director of the Leadership Council on Legal Diversity, which is a group of managing partners of the Am Law 200, the 200 largest firms in the country that are named in the *American Lawyer*, and the general counsel of Fortune 500 companies. He also serves on several community boards. Robert knows the advantage of taking risks and of moving to a different solution once a disappointment is encountered. His life is based on his authenticity as a human being and the service he can provide to others.

# PART 4
# Determination

# Adapt to Change

*Benes Z. Aldana*

Benes was born in a small town in the Philippines and when his parents came to the States when he was seven, he lived with his grandparents for three years. He came to the United States with his brothers when he was ten years old. He is from a very small town where everybody knew each other. He says, "My father's parents, particularly my grandmother, are the reason why we are here in the United States. She was a nurse and came in during an immigration wave when the United States was recruiting nurses. She settled in Pasadena, California, and after that petitioned my dad and his siblings to come to the United States. When my dad came to the United States, he joined the Navy and then the rest of us came along."

Being separated from your parents for over three years had to have been an eternity. The biggest defining moment of his life was his transition from the Philippines to the United States. He says, "The reason the plane ride was such a defining moment is because it was the beginning of self-awareness for me. I was beginning to know who I was, and I knew that there was this new adventure of a life full of possibilities and opportunities about to begin. I was either going to grab it or just continue on and take a different approach to life. I remember having my first steak, and it wasn't even that good of a steak, but I just devoured it. I remember that smell distinctly. But, I did get sick afterward. Our first entry was in Honolulu, Hawaii, on February 14, 1980. That's my anniversary of landing in the United States."

When Benes started school in the United States, he had a thick accent. His English was not very good. The kids at school made fun of him. He also got picked on for being Catholic, being taunted with, "Hey, you are not really a Christian." He was living on a Navy base, so it was probably more Protestant. He says, "I always felt the need to prove myself." To defend himself, he and his brothers pretended to know karate. It was almost an everyday ritual. They would get off the bus and some bully would be waiting to pick on them because of their accent. They would fake karate moves and the kids would scatter. He says, "I think as an immigrant you always want to continue to prove yourself and you are determined to do things better. You have to adapt to change. Improvise like we did with the karate in fifth grade." These experiences taught Benes how to deal with change and that often catapulted him ahead of his peers.

Benes really started to adapt in eighth grade and he continued to use his differences and his winning personality to get ahead in winning many contested student body elections. He recalls, "When I was in eighth grade we moved to Oak Harbor, Washington. It was a new junior high school and they were having fall elections for student body officers. I thought it would be fun to run for student body vice president. One of the candidates was complaining that I couldn't run because I was only in the eighth grade, but the student government advisor said I could run. As I was walking out the door after I filed the petition, I overheard him tell the other kids who were running, 'He doesn't know anybody; he's not going to win.' I just smiled to myself and went on. We gave our speeches at an assembly and they liked my speech and I won the election. I've always been a fan of President John Kennedy, so I channeled him in my message, and it worked. The following year, I was elected student body president. The same thing happened in college at Seattle University, which is an independent Jesuit university. I was the first Filipino to be elected as president in the college's history."

By this time Benes knew he wanted to become a lawyer, so he interned on Capitol Hill during his sophomore year in college. He says, "I knew that going to law school would be a powerful tool for making a difference, or at least empower me as a person to be a tool, an agent of change. I have a drive to leave the world a better place. I know that sounds corny and people either understand or they don't. I think some people have that DNA and some people don't."

His whole concept of adapting to change was really crystallized in high school when he was selected to be a part of a program called Governor's School. He says, "It's a great program to teach young people how to think about the issues of the day from the local perspective, state perspective, national, and international perspectives. And to learn to have conversations about topics that normally people don't talk about—racism, sexism, and all the 'isms'—to eliminate those kinds of issues and how to deal with them. During those four weeks, we were also assigned to a focus group, I was fortunate to be assigned to Bill Gates as my community leader. At the time, it was like—who is this Bill Gates guy? I wanted to be assigned to State Senator Gary Locke, who later became governor of Washington and secretary of commerce and ambassador to China. I was more interested in politics. I was so happy to have been in his group after all because one important message I came away with from having been in this focus group was the idea of adapting to change. It's good to have goals, dream big, think big, but be flexible enough to see other opportunities. People say that all the time, but Bill Gates said it, and it stuck in my mind. In everything I do I try to live up to that kind of message in terms of my career—being able to be flexible."

Learning this lesson so early helped Benes immensely in his military career. He started out as a trial counsel (military prosecution) in San Francisco and his first case as a young lawyer getting out of law school was a rape case in the military. After that he became an appellate government counsel in Washington, DC, and assumed charge of the Coast Guard's legal assistance program. Then he became deputy chief of the Coast Guard's environment law office.

One of his biggest defining moments was 9/11. It changed everyone's lives and it also changed the Coast Guard. Homeland Security was created and the Coast Guard became more at the center of protecting the homeland. He was getting on-the-job training and adapting to new roles. He was selected to serve as a legal advisor to the Department of Defense criminal investigation task force in Guantanamo Bay, Cuba, charged with investigating the detainees captured in the war on terrorism. He says, "Of all of my legal experience, that is probably the biggest defining moment because I had to use my morals and ethics in confronting the current issues of the day. I also believe the JAGS are the conscience of the military and during this experience, it definitely demonstrated that they are because it was the JAGS who raised some of those issues in Guantanamo, not going out to the media, but through proper channels to try to do the right thing. There was a tension between trying to protect our country and getting the best intelligence and at the same time, trying to establish justice. We were sorting out all the issues between combatant and noncombatant and determining whether or not the Geneva Convention applied to the detainees. Our task force was charged with looking at what war crimes were violated and trying to bring to justice those people who committed those crimes. There is a Senate Report that talks about what the JAGS did during that time."

Afterward he got a chance to promote rule of law and human rights in Africa. He became the person in charge of the US military's efforts to advance rule of law and human rights in Africa working with African militaries throughout Africa. His team, a legal team of professionals, lawyers, and paralegals, was in charge of making sure that the goals of advancing rule of law in human rights were achieved by promoting a program that focuses on civilian control of the military, preventing military corruption, and establishing accountability systems, to name a few. His station was all over Africa—Tanzania, South Sudan, and other countries. They worked with the military in training and teaching them about military justice, human rights and humanitarian law. He found that many countries in Africa saw us as the model in the world. Benes says, "That is one thing that I learned working and living abroad in Europe and travelling throughout Africa. The United States was seen as a model for freedom and democracy. That reputation has suffered in recent years."

After Africa, Benes became the district legal counsel for the Eighth Coast Guard District, which covers twenty-six states in dividing the Gulf of Mexico. He was the lawyer for the admiral in charge of the Eighth Coast Guard District. He has moved a lot since he joined the Coast Guard and ended up becoming the chief trial judge of the US Coast Guard—the first Asian Pacific American to serve as a chief trial judge in US military history. When he retired from the military, he was chosen to be the president of the National Judicial College, the nation's oldest, largest, and most prestigious educational institution for judges where he has his work cut out for him. Benes' life and career has exemplified the flexibility to adapt to change. I can't wait to see what's in store for him.

# The System Does Work

*Alan Yamamoto*

Alan was born in 1945, shortly after his parents came out of a Japanese internment camp in Poston, Arizona, where they were incarcerated along with their families. His parents ended up buying a farm in Watsonville, California, and Alan grew up "growing strawberries." But his parents' time in Arizona still impacted him throughout his life and influenced his commitment to justice for all, regardless of race, nationality, or creed. After finishing his undergraduate degree at Berkeley on a 1-S Deferment, Alan enlisted in Army intelligence and was shipped to Vietnam. "The war switched my sights from corporate law to doing legal services type work. I witnessed the suffering of the people there in Vietnam and the war did not make much sense to me. It changed my perspective."

Alan's first job out of law school was at the Cleveland Legal Aid Society in the Mental Health Unit, one of the first mental health units in the country. "At the time I joined, they were doing constitutional litigation and right to counsel cases, so we did right to counsel matters, and we were doing right to treatment cases." Alan and his team won the right to counsel. "So those persons who were having mental health commitment hearings had a right to counsel."

Unfortunately, the court decided to appoint counsel, effectively putting Alan out of a job. From there, he worked in neighborhood offices doing juvenile litigation and neighborhood legal assistance. "Eventually, I moved down to Washington and was hired by the Labor Department in the Solicitor's Office working with the Mine Safety & Health Administration (MSHA). That is the organization that regulates the mining industry." Shortly after, he went into private practice. "I decided I wanted to go off on my own and I quit. I opened up shop here in Virginia, and I've been practicing by myself since 1986." Like many new practitioners, Alan started taking whatever came in the door. Currently, he does primarily federal criminal work, with some wills and estates on the side. "I also represent some small corporations doing their corporate work."

Then, after Alan was finishing up a death penalty case with Judge Leonie Brinkema, the judge asked Alan into her chambers after a hearing one day. She told him she had a defendant who wanted to go *pro se,* and that his name popped into her head for the appointment. The client's name was Zacarias Moussaoui, a French citizen involved in the September 11 terrorist attacks. Alan asked Judge Brinkema if he could have the weekend to talk to his family about it. "I wanted to make sure my wife, my parents, my brothers, and sisters were okay with it." They all agreed, and Alan took on the new client, acting as standby counsel. Standby counsel is provided where a defendant has invoked his right to self-representation. "In this case, Mr. Moussaoui was going to represent himself and standby counsel is there to advise him if he requests advice and to help him manage his way through the courtroom. Counsel helps him with preparation of motions, explains to him what the court process is, and what the trial process is—if he was interested in using that advice."

Because of this new assignment, Alan ended up having to withdraw from the rest of the cases he was working on at the time. "The federal defenders were initially to be removed from the case, and they were looking for other counsel to help me as standby counsel. It ended up that no other law firm would pick up the case. The court ended up leaving the federal defenders on the case along with the other counsel, Ed MacMahon, who was on the case. We were all there." Alan's goal was to keep his client from receiving the death penalty. "He pled guilty to the indictment. The indictment carried mandatory life. The only issue was whether or not he was going to get the death penalty. He was given life, so we won."

During the trial, Alan says his life was a constant struggle every day. "I met with him seven days a week for almost four years. Eight hours a day, every day. We almost never talked about the case. He didn't want to talk about the case." What did they talk about? "Everything else.

Religion, current events, his family, my family." Was there any common ground? "Sure, there was a lot of common ground and a lot of things he believed I understood. I could sympathize with him or empathize. Ultimately, it wasn't until after the verdict that we felt vindicated because after the results, it looked like this giant light bulb went off over his head because he always felt that he was going to get the death penalty. He was making a mockery of the system. But when they came back eleven to one and the one was for not death, he saw that *the system does work*, and then he wanted a new trial."

Finally, Zacarias Moussaoui understood what his standby lawyer, Alan, had been trying to tell him from the beginning—the system does work, and it works for everyone. "The law is there for everyone, and certainly the less fortunate—sometimes they need it more than anybody else. The purpose of lawyers is to try to help those people."

# Failure Is Not an Option

*Cindy K. Hide*

Cindy grew up with a young, single, mother who had very little education. "When she divorced, she had a baby, a very young child, and no education, so she had to go back to school at night and worked during the day. Basically, she put herself on her feet with her own consulting business several years later." But during Cindy's formative years, that success was too far off to see clearly. "I grew up in a household that was a little rough. I really had a first-hand understanding of what it was like to be on your own as a woman and to appreciate the value of an education."

From a young age, Cindy had to learn how to not only take care of herself, but also take care of her younger sister as well. "In some ways, I suppose, that was the foundation for wanting to excel professionally because that was reinforced later when I was working my way through college waiting tables. I did all kinds of minimum wage, "break your back" type jobs. That was the clincher in my inspiration for going to law school. I thought, 'I am not doing this the rest of my life.' It was just too hard."

Law school wasn't an obvious choice for Cindy. She aspired to be a professional ballet dancer and had the talent to pursue it. Her mother told her that if she chose to earn a professional degree that she would pay for her tuition, regardless of which school she chose to attend. Cindy considered her options and went with continuing her education. She says she thought, "I better go to law school. I've always been interested in the law. Justice is something that strikes a deep chord with me. Truly, still, principle is probably the inside piece of who I am. I do things on principle. I try to conduct my life that way. I do my business that way. I raised my children that way. I have to be very clear and comfortable with anything that I'm doing or that I put my energy into before I move forward."

Due to Cindy's challenging circumstances during her upbringing, she strived not only to live by principle, but to have a happy, healthy, and functional family. Her first marriage didn't stick, but she was sure that her second one was *the* one. When they met, Cindy had already been practicing law a couple years. Her husband wanted to have children immediately because he was slightly older, and they both were eager to start a family. "When I got pregnant, I really thought my child was not going to interfere in my schedule because I had a law practice and I was going to go to work just like I did, come home, be a mom for a few hours, and then good night. My neighbor, by chance, was also pregnant and we had our kids within two weeks of each other. I thought, 'This is perfect. I'll just take my son next door and drop him off, so he can play with her baby. Then I'll come home.' Well, what happened was first we started at 8:00 a.m. Then it was 9:00 a.m. and I would come home at 5:00 or 6:00 p.m. Then I'd drop him at 10:00 a.m. and be at home by 4:00 p.m." Eventually it got to the point where Cindy started bringing her son to work with her. Then she decided to step out of the practice for a while to raise her son. Eighteen months later her daughter was born. "I just fell in love with my children and with being a mom."

After seventeen years of marriage, Cindy divorced. Out of that process came her first book, *Do I Stay or Do I Leave?* One of her defining moments came to her through the divorce process. She says, "It was early in our divorce. I had taken the kids on vacation and I thought that after having been married to someone for so many years that we could handle things amicably. I didn't bother to separate our joint accounts; I didn't bother to do anything that wasn't jointly owned. I didn't think we needed to do that. We were going to work through it. We had already started the divorce process, but when I came back with the children from a short trip, I came back to a bank account that had $125 in it. He had taken all the money out of our accounts, out of savings, had maxed the equity line on our home, and he had taken the credit cards and had locked me out of our business that we'd grown together for years during marriage. I had nothing."

Cindy's first round of attorney's fees was loaned by her father. Shortly thereafter, those monies were exhausted and she had no way to hire representation. Her expert wouldn't stick around without proper financing either, and she was an emotional wreck. At a hearing on this issue, she stood there alone while her husband was surrounded by lawyers and supporters. She told the court she had no experience in family law and that she didn't want to represent herself. The female judge denied her request for attorney fees and said she would award them at the end of the case and only if there was an equitable division of their assets. Cindy was shocked. "I was so absorbed with 'what in the world am I going to do?' while at the same time I was determined that this should not happen to any other woman who had put her family first."

Cindy felt that she was living out her worst nightmare. But she persevered, she refused to quit fighting. "I decided to move back to Houston to start over. Houston is home. It's not an easy road but thank God I have a law degree, thank God I had prepared myself, and to that I'll give credit to my history living through the life I had growing up with my mother and seeing how she struggled by not having an education. I'll give her big credit for that."

Moving forward, Cindy became extremely proactive in her quest for justice because of her experience. "I decided I was going to create a place where women can go to learn, to get education, about all the different elements of what it takes substantively, emotionally, and financially, to get through a very contentious transition in divorce." She started getting in touch with her spiritual center and held multidisciplinary conferences, that included experts from finance, law, psychology, and spirituality. "We had a whole day of women. It was so successful." The conferences grew in popularity, and Cindy started fielding sponsorship offers from national corporations.

Through all of Cindy's life, she's seen downfalls, she's faced them, and she's used them to create something wonderful. "Failure to me would be that I don't get the word out about the knowledge and experience I have. It's part of becoming an elder. I'm not thirty years old any more. Getting through the last thirty years of experiences means something and you have to give back and help someone avoid a misstep or help them slow down enough to think carefully about their decisions. My tough times are not going to be wasted."

# Your Possibilities Are Limitless

*Scott C. LaBarre*

Scott was born in St. Paul, Minnesota, and grew up in Woodbury, Minnesota, and his life embodies the principle of determination because he has overcome the disability of being blind as a lawyer and has never let that stop him from moving forward or achieving his goals. He says, "I've always looked up to my dad. He has always been a great supporter of mine and he, along with my mom, always wanted to make sure that we children had more opportunities than they had. Neither of my parents has anything beyond a high school diploma, and they have always had to work very hard to earn middle income status."

Margins were lean in Scott's early years and his father did most of the work around the house. Scott remembers getting to help him and his friends pour the concrete for the foundation. Scott's father instilled in him the principle of being responsible for his own life. He says, "I learned to just get out there when I had an idea, a dream, or an ambition and go for it, even though it appeared the odds were stacked against me." Scott's mom was a secretary and then took off to be a stay-at-home mom when he was young. He remembers her teaching him to read and how much he loved reading. Especially books about aviation and space travel. He wanted to be a pilot.

There was nothing remarkable about his health as a young child. He was just a normal boy. But in the fourth grade, he contracted retinitis uveitis and had to learn to deal with and adjust to the new reality of being blind. He had a bunch of surgeries on his left eye and then after enduring a lot of pain, he lost it. At that time, he thought he still had his right eye.

He got special tutoring to catch up in school from a favorite teacher named Mr. Hebzenski. Scott says, "All the parents thought he was a terrible teacher because he wasn't very polished. I remember he was extremely dedicated. This was an important life lesson to me because I remember people being very judgmental of Mr. Hebzenski just because he had this rough façade and acted tough, uncouth, and blue-collar. That turned a lot of people off and they thought he wasn't a good teacher, but it taught me that you should never underestimate people. You should never give great weight to what the outside packaging is, and you should never be quick to judge anybody else. I didn't think of it in those terms when I was nine years old, but it was an important lesson to me because if it had not been for him I would have been delayed a year and maybe I would have never had the passion to apply myself in respect to schooling."

A year later, in fifth grade, his other eye started giving him problems and the virus was back. He had to stay in the hospital for weeks in Baltimore to get testing to see if they could save his other eye. Scott remembers the spinal tap as the worst. He left Johns Hopkins on a "wing and a prayer" and they tried some new drugs, but they did not work. He got the bad news that he was going to lose his right eye, too. The doctor finally told him he had to get used to the fact that he was going to be blind.

Scott never wanted his blindness to limit him. He remembers coming home from the hospital and his mother set a bowl of lasagna down in front of him. He says, "I thought to myself, 'Am I helpless all of a sudden? What is this? You don't eat lasagna out of a bowl.' Well, my mom never did that again because she realized that she should not treat me any differently. The first night was like somebody died in our family. Everybody was just totally depressed. I think the reason I was so scared and overwhelmed is because the portrait of blindness that I had as a child that was reinforced by shows like *Sesame Street* and popular media, was that blind people were the ones that stood on street corners and sold pencils and begged for charity. The typical blind person had a guide dog and dark sunglasses. That was my image of blindness."

Scott was supposed to be a pilot. And he had talent as an artist. He drew *Star Wars* pictures. And now he realized he could not do any of that anymore. He says, "After the first initial blow, my parents realized that life had to get back to normal, a new normal perhaps, but it had to get back to normal. They contacted the people they needed to contact, and I went right back to school. I started learning braille immediately. They put a white cane into my hands. They did so because I pretty much lost almost all of my vision. I consider myself lucky that I went blind that way. Starting in the 1970s Congress said you need to give blind kids mainstream education. You need to bring the special educational elements into the classroom—this concept of 'full inclusion.' I was in the first couple of years of that change in education. They kept me at Royal Oaks Elementary with my peers that I had been going through school with ever since kindergarten. What I ended up doing is spending an hour or two a day with this vision teacher learning braille, learning adaptive techniques, learning whatever it was I needed to learn. The reason I say I am lucky about the way I went blind is I, as an advocate and somebody deeply involved in the blindness field now, have observed the great loss of many years by people who live in the 'netherworld.'"

The most amazing thing about Scott was that while he under-achieved in his first few years of elementary school, going blind really turned him around. He says, "When I went blind, I realized something had to change. I realized that people were going to regard me as something less than or something broken. I knew I needed to start trying a lot harder, and I did. From that fifth-grade year on, I was always an A student."

Scott attended Saint John's University in Minnesota, which is a small private Catholic liberal arts school. He won a scholarship to college from the National Federation of the Blind. He remembers, "I thought I was a pretty exceptional, hotshot blind guy. I was going to go down to this convention of blind people and teach them something. What happened is I learned a lot. I finally met blind people who were role models; people that I could look up to. I did not know one blind adult between the age of ten until I was eighteen or so; only one blind adult who was holding down a job."

The federation turned out to be his other family. He says, "Those two families have conspired or contributed to making me who I am now. I was fascinated by the concept that blind people are treated as second-class citizens in our society." He became a government major and that led him to the law. He attended the University of Minnesota Law School.

Scott is really tough-minded about his blindness and really lives by his LEAD line: "Your possibilities are limitless." He remarked about law school, "In terms of dealing with my blindness there really was not a problem because by the time I was in law school I had developed a lot of techniques and alternatives to doing things visually and I did not have a barrier there. A lot of people say to me, 'Law school must have been so tough for you.' What they are saying is, 'Law school must have been so tough for you because you are blind.' Isn't law school tough for anybody? I didn't ask for anything special; I didn't make any excuses, because of my blindness. Yes, I had accommodations. I used braille. But I was busy because I became president of the National Association of Blind Students. I spent a great deal of time working to build that organization and travelling throughout the country and doing advocacy for blind students."

He doesn't like to be treated like there is something special about him. He says, "The thing I hate is when people say to me, 'You are amazing. You're so courageous,' when they don't know anything personally about me. Maybe I am amazing; maybe I am courageous; but it's not just because I can get off my seat and walk to the door. This whole concept of 'You are amazing for doing things that are so simple and just routine' is nuts. I'm not amazing because of that; I'm amazing because of what I've accomplished and what I do with my life as a person. My blindness is an integral part of who I am; it formed my personality; it taught me a lot of things and continues to teach me a lot of things; but I am not amazing just because I can walk from my chair to a door or I can travel through airports."

Scott always finds a way to turn a negative into the positive, and his sheer drive and desire to innovate and create a brilliant life make him someone I admire. He is deeply involved in the National Federation of the Blind, one of whose key themes is braille literacy. And he will soon take the seat at the officers table at GPSolo and one day will be chair of the division. He is also completing a three-year term on the ABA Board of Governors and serves as president of the National Association of Blind Lawyers. He's come a long way, and nothing will limit his possibilities.

# Define Your Path and Fulfillment Will Follow

*Laura V. Farber*

Laura was born in Buenos Aires, Argentina, during a very tumultuous time in the stability of the government. Both of her parents were PhD candidates at the University of Buenos Aires. Laura's dad has told her time and again the story of when they decided to move to the States—Laura's mom was meant to be doing some class experiments in a lab but wasn't feeling well and went back to their apartment. That same day, a tear gas raid was done at the lab. "The military folks didn't like students because students always criticized the government and if you criticized the government your voice needed to be silenced," she says. Laura's dad thought that Laura's mom was still at the laboratory and went into the biggest panic he had ever experienced. She says, "He decided that day that they would be leaving the country. Some way, somehow, they would leave the country." Fortunately, a shared mentor had a connection in the States, and her parents were able to come to the United States, "with absolutely nothing, except for me in tow, and they started a new life."

Laura's grandfather was a lawyer in Argentina. "He was the kind of man who was driven by principle. He would take any matter that came in because he was that main street lawyer, believe it or not, who just wanted to help people." She tells the story of a particular time her grandfather went above and beyond to help his clients. "Divorce was not something you could do in Argentina since it is a Catholic country. It had a national religion. These people came in, and one of them wanted a divorce. He said that he could not legally help them with a divorce. They could do what is, I guess, a separation. He talked the people into getting back together. And he didn't get any money out of it. He was so driven by what he felt was right and what he thought would be helpful in human relationships. He was not a good businessman by any stretch, but he really got a lot of fulfillment out of what he did. He said to me, 'I hope you have the chance if this is the path you choose to take, to make a difference, and to always remember what is important.' I carried that with me." I assumed this was the driving force in her career path, but she set me straight. She told me she wasn't even responsible for making the decision that she would go to law school.

While Laura was in college, she assumed she would go into science based on the fact that her parents are biochemists. "Everybody in my family is in science." Her freshman year at UCLA, Laura realized that while she was talented in physics, she wasn't passionate about it. "I decided I needed to start doing other things, and I ended up being a political science major with a business emphasis. Through that, I used my grandfather as an example, but I don't think I really knew that I was going to go into the law until maybe my sophomore year of college. That's when I started thinking, "You know what? This could be an area that I could pursue here. Maybe there is a path I can take that will help people.""

Laura attended Georgetown Law, where one professor left her with a bitter taste in her mouth. "I saw this law professor humiliate the women in my class. He picked on them." She was indignant. "His goal was to make the women in his class cry." Laura was infuriated by his teaching methods, and that feeling stayed with her long after his class ended. "It gave me a strong sense of fairness and what's right and what isn't. How dare he attack people's dignity and their self-respect? Having these women question whether they were even qualified to be there. It's outrageous. There is no place for that. It really did trigger this sense of fairness I have in me today."

Once Laura graduated, she knew that regardless of where she was practicing law, she had to make sure she was doing something that helped people in bad situations. She says, "I admire the people in the trenches that are doing this day in and day out. I did toy with public interest early on, but realized I wasn't sure I could do it. I think that was probably what drove me to make sure that I did some bar-related work with some *pro bono*. That completes me. That fulfills me. I could not practice law without doing the public servant work."

Currently, Laura is one that many would consider to be "in the trenches." She works in employment law and also does personal injury. She's not above taking a slip and fall, but she does try to seek out the cases where she can really make a difference. "I had this family, a Latino family, whose parents were janitors at Cal Tech. They were killed by a drunk driver who collided with them, and their car burned and exploded. I represented the kids of this family in a wrongful death claim. It was another powerful case, especially the depositions. I had never had that experience before where kids were telling the stories and showing the photos. Can you imagine your parents being yanked from you in that horrible way? I had to take a deposition at the Coalinga State Prison. I had never done that before."

Laura is certainly headstrong and determined, and looks for ways she can "be the change." It's driven her to tough cases, and it's driven her to be involved in the American Bar Association and other community service. She chaired the Young Lawyers Division. And, she's the first Latina to serve as president of the Tournament of Roses and only the third woman. "It's not something I sought or positioned myself to do. I just love this group and it was something I did growing up." Moving forward, it's almost a given that Laura will continue to drive forward and astound all those around her. She lives by the example her grandfather set for her back in Argentina.

# Practice Empathy

*Christopher L. Griffin*

Chris lives in Tampa, Florida. His story is all about empathy. Growing up, Chris was passionate about equality. He recognized from an early age that racial equality was one of the country's most pressing problems. It led him to becoming fascinated with the law, which led him to go to law school. Along with that was a family-fueled passion for community activity. "My dad was always involved in community activities and it was just part of what I wanted to do as a citizen."

In high school, Chris was president of the student body and captain of the football team. However, things changed dramatically when his high school was integrated. For Chris, this was a dream come true—the two best football teams in the district merged into one, and he was at the center of the action. The team was so successful that their games were scheduled for Saturday, while everyone else played on Friday, so that the whole town could attend. However, Chris soon realized that the new students at his school were not pleased to be there. He remembers a pep rally at the football stadium when the black students crowded in the end-zone. He looked down and thought, "This is wrong."

The high school they had been transferred out of had been the center of their community for more than a hundred years, and they were suddenly uprooted and placed in an unfamiliar environment. As excited as Chris had been for the changes brought by integration, in that moment he empathized with the new students. He became passionate about racial equality. "There was something ingrained in our household culture that racism was wrong." The empathy

Chris felt toward his new classmates guided him throughout much of his education and career.

"I can never remember a moment when I didn't want to be a lawyer." Chris's father was a lawyer, and later a judge, but didn't attend law school until he was forty years old, graduating when Chris was eight. "When my father went to law school, I lived through law school." Chris credits both his parents as being strong role models. "I have always been attracted to standing up and speaking on behalf of something or someone." His mother especially shaped the way he approached his career. "My mother supported the family for the years my father went to law school, and then she stayed in the teaching profession because she was a good teacher and she loved it. I saw a woman who didn't need to work to support the family, but who wanted to stay in her profession because it was what fulfilled her."

In college Chris was a political science major. An exciting life-changing event happened the summer between his sophomore and junior years; it was the summer of 1974. It was a momentous summer in the history of the country. He was a congressional intern to Lawton Chiles, a senior senator who later served as governor. In 1973, Sam Ervin's Watergate Committee was held and in the summer of 1974 the House Impeachment Committee met. Chris and eight of his fellow interns slept on the steps of the Supreme Court to hear the arguments between the Watergate Special Counsel, Leon Jaworski, from the law firm of Fulbright, Freeman, Bates and Jaworski, and a guy named James St. Clair from Boston who represented the president in the Tapes Case. The issue was whether President Nixon had to turn over the Oval Office tape recordings.

The lines were getting long so they came up with an idea to enforce their own numbering system, and everyone agreed. By the middle of the night, there were more than two hundred people there. The Supreme Court guards enforced their system. They walked them across the street in groups of ten. They got to see the entire argument. *The New York Times* ran a front-page photo of them. The experience solidified his interest in the law.

As a lawyer, Chris's early life shaped much of his work. His father's dedication to service and his mother's dedication to her career led him to become active in the ABA. He worked himself up in the ranks of the Young Lawyers Division to become Chair in 1987 to 1988. I asked what his big burning issue during his year as Chair of the Young Lawyers Division was. He says, "Specifically, gender discrimination within the practice of law and in the justice system. I think I saw it as another form of injustice, but it was one that I could identify with more because of the racial equality issue—I could never know what it was truly like to be a black person. I certainly don't know what it was like to be a woman, but a little closer in I just sensed there was not as much awareness and sensitivity of the issue as there was racial discrimination, and I thought it was something that really needed our attention."

Chris's mentor was a woman, and he credits her with teaching him how to practice law. He saw her experience sexism on many different levels, and that inspired him to make a change in the playing field. One moment that stands out was at his first law firm, a female client came in to seek the firm's services. She was adamant that she did not want a woman on her case, to the point that she went to another law firm and found another lawyer. Again, his empathy kicked in and the situation motivated him to take action.

As his career continued, he became more involved in gender issues. He was asked to be on the Commission on Women in the Profession at a time when Hillary Clinton was the Chair. "I thought I understood the issue of women's rights and sexual or gender discrimination, but I sure didn't. I learned later because I went on that commission and that's when my life changed in terms of seeing women's issues in a certain way." During his time on the Commission on Women in the Law, Chris learned meaningful lessons. First, it was suggested that the Commission give a special award to and have a keynote speech by Anita Hill. "I and one other member of the Commission argued that that was a very impolitic thing to do and that the ABA had already taken enough grief from its membership on the *Roe v. Wade* resolution. The last thing we wanted to do was pick a public fight because we said if you give the award to Anita Hill, you are essentially saying that the Justice of the Supreme Court is a liar. That's what I argued. And I said, 'Do you really want to do that?'" The vote was no.

The backlash was bigger than Chris could have anticipated. He recalls one friend who was so upset with him she could barely look at him. He finally confronted her, and she told him, "'You have no idea what Anita Hill has become to the women of America.'" He says, "And the way she put it to me was, 'I'm the one who takes the phone calls from women who have been the subject or have been subjected to what Anita Hill claims she was subjected to.'"

Chris's friend told him just how drastically calls from women had increased, asking for legal advice about similar situations. He says,

"I was blown away because I didn't understand it on the emotional level and she got me to thinking about a woman who is discriminated against, who is sexually harassed, and who can't do anything about it because the rules of the game are if you speak up about it, you're going to be ostracized, and that's exactly what happened to Anita Hill."

Chris continued to be an advocate for women. He says, "I make it a very important part of the way I run my law practice that the female associates in my department are treated equally. In fact, we pay attention to the lingering aspects of gender discrimination. I make sure that I walk the walk as well as talk the talk in my law practice."

After the Commission on Women in the Law, he chaired the Domestic Violence Commission. "After a few years of catching my breath, I then went on the board of the local governing group for our local Domestic Violence Shelter." Throughout everything, he has remained very involved in the ABA.

Chris's life has not been one of pure success. He has had his share of ups and downs, but things have always worked out for the best and he is able to see that in the long run. He tried several times for judgeships on the federal level during the Clinton administration and the Obama administration, but was not appointed. He says, "It's a huge emotional investment to put yourself out there when you feel you are accomplished and that you have a lot to offer and then to be told 'no.' I respect people who apply for positions and make that investment of their own emotions and time. The thing I can say about the Commission both during the Clinton and the Obama administrations, the people that they put on the bench are first-rate people so I'm like, 'Well, I tried, but the people who got it are really good, so what else can I ask for?'"

Life handed him another opportunity that has actually been very rewarding. "Because of my sports background, I was a football player in college, and my appellate experience, I was asked to join the Infractions Appeals Committee for Division I of the NCAA as a public member, and I became the chairman. The National Collegiate Athletic Association is the governing body for all intercollegiate athletics in the United States." They look at all rules and infractions committed by coaches and athletes and schools in the country—recruitment, academic fraud by athletes to name a few.

Setback or no setback, Chris will continue to practice empathy and to fight for what he believes in.

# Persistence Pays Off

*Kent W. Spence*

Kent was raised by a lawyer, Gerry Spence, but the thought never occurred to him to follow in his father's footsteps until he had been a carpenter for six years after high school. He says, "I carpentered all over Wyoming from Riverton to Jackson to Laramie to Lander to Fort Washakie. I even went to California." From age nineteen to twenty-four, he followed a guru, Guru Maharaja. "I meditated and lived an austere life, and I would be a carpenter to support myself. Then I was involved with this group meditating and eating vegetarian and no meat, no women, or anything." Kent still meditates from time to time, but he stopped fasting from meat or women a long time ago. And he loves the law.

Kent could not go straight to law school because he had yet to attend college. He says, "I had really not been exposed to the law because the law that my dad was doing when I was younger did not inspire me; it just sounded boring." However, while he was working on some construction at his father's office, Kent started listening in on meetings his dad was having with these "so-called lawyers" that had brought him a case. "What these guys were doing sounded exciting. Taking on Kerr-McGee Corporation, the nuclear giant. I thought, 'I could spend the rest of my life being a carpenter. If I was a lawyer, I could go fight for the rights of people.' So that was my defining moment when I thought I could really make a difference out there."

Kent went to college a month later at the University of Montana. "I didn't have to take the SAT or anything." He was twenty-four years old and tested at an eighth-grade reading level. "It wasn't that I wasn't bright; I just had a poor education," he says. He worked on it. Kent went to a reading lab every day for an hour his entire first semester of college. By the end of it, he was testing at a reading level of a freshman in college. "I set my mind to it like I did everything else, and I graduated from the University of Montana with honors."

After graduation, Kent found his dad's work a little less boring. He spent a year between undergrad and law school doing investigative work and had an overall great experience. He moved down to the Deep South and attended Walter F. George School of Law at Mercer University. He took the bar, failed, then took it again and failed the multi-state by one point. He had heard of Peter Lewis, a bar tutor and South Texas College of Law professor, who was teaching the multi-state. "I lived in Houston for six weeks, and I studied with this guy twelve to fourteen hours a day. I came back to Wyoming and got the highest grade in the state on the multi-state."

I had to ask—did he ever feel like he would rather just quit? Kent was honest with me. "Sure," he said, "After all of that, after going through seven years of upper education for this dream to be a lawyer, I just couldn't give up over barely missing the exam a few times." Once he succeeded, "Oh my God, it was the most joyous day of my life. I was finally going to be a lawyer. I could finally practice law, instead of living this fiction in law school. I could actually represent people and go do what my dream was all about in the first place, which was fighting for the rights of people."

And fight for the rights of people he has. "In my career, I've done a lot of civil rights cases where I've sued police departments." Notably, in March 2009, Kent brought a case against the Precinct One constable in Houston, who hog-tied a mentally ill man who was schizophrenic, tasered him eighteen times, and ultimately broke his neck and suffocated him to death. Kent, co-counseling with Rafe Foreman and Susan Hutchinson, won a multi-million dollar verdict.

Looking back on his dad's "boring work," Kent now has a higher sense of appreciation of what his father was doing. Early out of law school, he had the opportunity to co-counsel some cases with his father. "I just said, 'Look, I get the chance to work with Gerry Spence. How many people in this country, how many young lawyers in this country, would love this opportunity?' They would carry his briefcase. I don't care if he is my dad. I have to take the hat off being his son and put on the hat of the young associate trying to learn how to be a good lawyer."

As for that construction remodel he was working on when he was first bit by an interest in the law? It is now the home of Trial Lawyers College, created by Gerry Spence at the family ranch. It's still around today—"It's a rigorous kind of boot camp living out at the ranch, living in dorm rooms, and working morning, afternoon, and evening every day." Kent has taught there as a staff member since 1996, sits on the board of directors and is still heavily involved to this day. Currently, the college has over 1,000 alumni around the country. The program teaches a lot of lessons that Kent seems to have grown up with. "We just get down to being vulnerable and real, and that's who we really are as human beings. We put on all these layers of what a great lawyer acts like, which covers up who we really are, and who we really are is just like everyone else. We have feelings. We have heart. We have gut-level reactions."

Today, Kent is still fighting for the rights of the people. He's still extremely active—He climbed Mt. Kilimanjaro when he turned 50. "I would say that I have continued to fight hard throughout my whole career to become better and better and better, and to become more successful. As it stands right now, I've been the president of the Wyoming Trial Lawyers Association, and I'm on the board of the Trial Lawyers College. I'm listed as one of the Top 100 Lawyers in Wyoming, and I continue to overcome serious battles all over the country." His goal always has been, and remains today, to "fight for the rights of people against big power."

His persistence has paid off. He never quit and is now enjoying a successful life with meaning.

# You Determine Your Own Success

*Scott E. Rozzell*

Scott grew up in the 1950s in a small town near Texarkana. When I asked him to tell me about his early life, he had one story that really shaped his life to share: He was about ten years old and he came home from school upset about something. He said to his mother, "Nobody likes me." Scott had a great mom who was a great inspiration and guidepost for him. He says, "I think even at that age I halfway expected to hear a sympathetic mother say, 'Oh, dear. You know that's not right. Everybody likes you. You're a wonderful child.' But instead, she looked me right in the eyes and said, 'Well, what are you going to do about that?'"

For Scott, it was a huge revelation. He says, "She was telling me that I was really in control of my own life. I was the person who made the decisions, and if I didn't like the way things were going, then it was up to me to try to change those. If there was something I wanted to accomplish, it was up to me to seek that out." It was a life-changing moment for him. He remembers it as vividly as if it happened yesterday, and he says he passed that same lesson on to his kids.

His father was in the lumber business and moonlighted as the town's mayor for twenty-eight years. I asked if that is what got him interested in politics. "Maybe less interested in politics," he said, "than sort of accepting the notion that you were supposed to give back to your community. I thought when you moved into a community you became involved in things that were important to your profession and to your community and that you participated in and contributed to those."

Scott realized that it was more about receiving—as a member of a community he felt it was required of him to give back, whether through church, organizations, or some sort of public service. Although that didn't directly impact his choice to attend law school, it certainly played a part. Scott has always wanted to be a problem-solver. "I thought lawyers were people who solved problems. I had gone to high school in the 1960s, during the civil rights movement; I had gone to a segregated high school; I saw the changes that were taking place in the country and noticed that lawyers played a prominent role. It was during the turmoil around the Vietnam War and lawyers were in the public debate on that issue. There were other significant issues of the day, and the common denominator was that lawyers were always right there in the thick of it. That appealed to me. Most of the problems that appeared to be important at that time were problems that I saw lawyers working on. I thought I wanted to be one of those."

Once he graduated law school and passed the bar, Scott continued to be active in many organizations, because "I thought that's what lawyers were supposed to do." Scott became president of Houston Young Lawyers Association and then president of the Houston Bar Association and then chaired the Texas Bar Foundation to name a few. His prolific leadership and stellar career are an example to all. He says, "I thought lawyers were supposed to be active in their bar association. I didn't feel like it was an imposition on me to do that. I just thought that was part of what made one a lawyer, being involved with the bar and with other lawyers. I found that enormously satisfying over the years; getting a chance to be around a lot of lawyers that otherwise I wouldn't have an opportunity to meet, and I confess I like lawyers. I think they're fascinating people, and I've enjoyed that part of my life."

Speaking of lawyers, Scott seems to resent our public personas. If our calling ever needed a new public relations team, I'd be sure to call Scott. "Lawyers are not always held in high regard by the public. Sometimes that cynicism on the part of the public is justified. It always made me feel good because I thought much of the criticism aimed at lawyers is not justified."

Scott spent much of his early years at the law firm of Baker Botts in Houston. He recalls, "Baker Botts was an establishment firm and had a very good reputation across the practice areas. At that time, they represented many of the financial institutions and energy companies based in Houston. Plus, they made their law firm, which at that time almost one hundred fifty years old and had its start representing the railroads and a lot of the moneyed interests for the money centers in the east in Texas, from a blue-chip client list. I think anyone would be lucky to have a chance to represent those companies and individuals that were on that list."

Scott says this in answer to my question about how he went from being an energy lawyer to becoming general counsel to CenterPoint Energy, which is the second largest combined electric and gas utility company in the country: "Baker Botts had a program that allowed you to work in different parts of the firm, and I did work in different parts of them for the first several months. This is one of my defining moments. I remember being in my office working on an estate tax matter late on a Friday afternoon, and I got a call from the partner who said, 'We have a temporary injunction hearing on Monday, and I need some help over the weekend.' He didn't try to lie to me; he didn't say, 'Well, you're the best guy,' or 'You're the person I really wanted to work with;' I think I was probably the only person he could find, and he said, 'I need for you to stay and work this weekend.' I agreed and worked on a dispute involving a couple of energy companies and the allocation of petroleum products, which at that time was subject to government control. I really thought it was fascinating, and I worked on that matter and then the follow-up after the TRO hearing, the follow-up temporary injunction hearing and a few more items for that particular client. The partner really liked the work that I did, and I started doing more work in that area. Before I knew it, I was an energy lawyer. I've been one ever since."

The defining moments of our life come in all shapes and sizes and for Scott to be the one who was there, the one who showed up, his destiny was handed to him that weekend.

One of the areas of service Scott appreciated the most was his work on the Texas Commission for Lawyer Discipline. He says, "One of the things I've enjoyed most, or perhaps got the most satisfaction from, was chairing the Texas Commission for Lawyer Discipline, which is the top of the grievance system in Texas. I'm proud of the lawyers in Texas, and I'm proud of the way that we discipline ourselves. We do, I think, a very good job of addressing some of the common problems that lawyers are guilty of and some of the uncommon ones, too. Much better, I think, than most of the other professional organizations. I know for a fact that there are bad actors out there among the lawyers that we are unable to catch or discipline in the way that we might want, but despite those deficiencies, I think the system works well and does a good job of protecting the public and policing the ranks of lawyers."

Scott is retired now and is still flying World War II planes and heading up the board of the new flight museum in Houston. On flying he says, "People have always asked me when I became interested in airplanes and the answer to that is, I don't ever remember not being interested in airplanes. When I was in kindergarten back in 1955, they didn't teach you to write your name; they taught you colors and shapes. On my lunch pail and on my little cubby where you kept things, you got to put a symbol. An airplane was my symbol. I was fascinated by airplanes; I wanted to learn how to fly and when I became old enough to do so, I did. I first started when I was sixteen. I got my pilot's license when I was seventeen. I worked at an airport and that's the way they paid me; they taught me how to fly. After I had to start paying for it myself, I couldn't afford it, so I didn't fly from about the time I was nineteen until I had been practicing law about three or four years. I had a little money and convinced my then wife that it was a lot better to fly an hour and a half to see grandma with two screaming kids as opposed to driving for seven hours with two screaming kids. We bought a little airplane and I've been flying regularly ever since. In the early 1990s I started flying WWII vintage airplanes. I bought one and started flying in air shows and I've been flying in air shows probably twenty years now."

Scott grew up in a town built around a World War II Defense Plant, so all the streets in his town were named after WWII battles and heroes. The town was built in 1941 and 1942 and all of the streets were named after martyred heroes and glorious defeats. For instance, his elementary school was on Arizona Avenue, named after the battleship that was sunk at Pearl Harbor. His best friend lived on Singapore Drive, the British bastion that had been captured by the Japanese. The baseball field was on Burma Road. The house that he was born in was on a street called Luzon, which is an island in the Philippines. But the city was dedicated on June 8, 1942, and on June 4, 1942, the Americans won the battle of Midway. They immediately renamed the street Midway and he grew up at 412 Midway.

I asked him how it felt to fly those old World War II planes. He says, "It's a great experience flying these old airplanes for several reasons.

First of all, just the physical thrill of flying one is great. Second, you feel like you've been entrusted with an historic artifact. Third, you can feel what it must have been like to have been a young man or a young woman, because in the United States we had young women who flew those airplanes as well, although not in combat; what it must have been like for them to do something like that. That's a great experience. I've also had in the twenty years I've been doing this an opportunity to meet, and in some cases, become really good friends with some of the people who were my heroes when I was growing up. When I grew up, all my heroes were fighter pilots, and I had a chance to get to know some of them pretty well, and that's really been great."

Adding it all up—taking 100 percent responsibility for your life, being and staying involved, removing the film of cynicism often placed over lawyers' personas—how does Scott maintain his sense of optimism? "I've had enough ups and downs in my life. I lost a wife, Michelle, to breast cancer. But I am now happily married to my wife, Karen, who is a lawyer too and am living my dream of traveling the world with her."

But he always takes it back to his mother's wisdom. "I would tell young people . . . they have and should take control over their own lives. They need to determine what they want to do. They need to understand that they are the ones who have the most control over their own accomplishments. It's up to them to make their own way. The essential determinant of how you're going to do in your life is you. No one else."

# Don't Get Discouraged, Believe in the Law

*Richard "Racehorse" Haynes*

Racehorse lived a full life until April 28, 2017, when he passed at the age of ninety. His celebrated legal career spawned books, TV movies, and much publicity but he was the most humble and unassuming man you will ever meet. He was a true Texan through and through. I interviewed him when he was well into his eighties and still going strong in his office. He was truly a "lawyer's lawyer." When I walked in for the interview, I saw he and I both have a similar quirky habit—we hang our name tags from the various events we attend from a hook in our office and clip-them one by one to each other to make a conglomeration that grows bigger and bulkier every year. We both valued the time we give to our causes and were proud of the work we do. Seeing those tags every day is a reminder that what I do everyday has meaning. It's worth the blood, sweat, and tears.

Richard "Racehorse" Haynes graduated from law school in 1956 when things were very different than they are today. He walked into his first trial a couple of days later and accidentally kicked a spittoon on the way to address the jurors. Yes, they had spittoons in the courtroom back in those days. He noted how the jurors laughed at his clumsiness and he knew he had them. His vulnerability was what they loved, and they believed him throughout the trial. He told me that he kept up the practice of accidentally kicking the spittoon at each trial until one judge got wise and moved it. He told me that doing something that shows the jurors that you are human is what will bond you to them for the duration of the trial.

Racehorse went on to win a long string of criminal trials that gave him one of the longest winning streaks in legal history. His rise to fame really began in the 1970s with several highly publicized trials of high-profile members of society. Many of his legal strategies were unconventional but effective. He could concoct a theory, no matter how outrageous, and sell it to a jury like no other. He was always prepared, kind, and present, and he had a sense of humor like no one else. This complex, yet down-to-earth man was so loved by the legal community.

Racehorse was famous for his cross-examination. If the prosecution failed to bring a witness to trial, he was known to cross an empty chair. He says, "You just have to watch the jury to see if they are getting the message—the SOB is lying, and if he's lying about one thing, he's going to lie about all things."

When I asked him about picking jurors, he told me, "I try to pick jurors that I think can be sympathetic, and I examine them pretty carefully and make sure I don't have a bad juror. I remember one time, I was trying a case and I felt sure my client was innocent. He was accused of stealing money from the bank where he worked, and they found him not guilty. I told him that if they found him not guilty, to get up and thank the jury. He got up and said, 'I want to thank you ladies and gentlemen, and I'll never do it again.' After that I wouldn't let anybody say anything to the jury."

One of his more notorious cases was the defense of Dr. John Hill. Dr. Hill was accused of killing his wife, Joan Hill. Racehorse got a mistrial in the first trial and Joan Hill's father, Ash Robinson, allegedly hired a guy to shoot Dr. Hill before he could be tried again. Racehorse remembered, "Tommy Thompson wrote a good book about it, *Blood and Money*. It was a well-written book. I wish I had read it again. I could remember more of the case. I knew Dr. Hill and he had done some surgery on my daughter. I knew he was a good doctor."

After John Hill was shot before his second trial, Racehorse tried to win a civil case against Ash Robinson. Racehorse said, "When we were taking Ash Robinson's deposition, he and I went to the potty. Ash said, 'You know I did it, don't you?' I said, 'Yeah, I do.' He said, 'You've got to prove it.' I said, 'I know it.' We sued him, but I couldn't prove it.'" I'm sure he wished he tried that case in today's time where phones could record conversations. That would have been a slam dunk!

Another famous case Racehorse tried was the Cullen Davis case. Racehorse recalls, "You've got to remember that Cullen was an Aggie and he was the son of a multimillionaire. He had a brother who was sharing the multimillions with him, and he had this great big house in Fort Worth right on the golf course, Columbia Golf Course. He married a gal that was anxious to be part of Fort Worth society, and she was cheating around on him. He got a divorce and she cheated him in the divorce. She got the house and a lot of money and property. I didn't think he was guilty of the killings. I knew he had been at the movies that night because he described the movie. I personally went over and talked to the man who worked at the movie theater who saw him come in, checked him in, and even showed me where he sat. I knew he was innocent."

Racehorse's sense of humor comes out in the next part about the trial that he shared: "The only thing funny that happened during Cullen's trial in Amarillo was I got a lot of mail from people because there was a lot of press. I got one letter from Odessa, a little town outside of Amarillo. It said, 'I am praying for you and doing everything I can to help you. Yours truly, God.' The letter had a phone number, so I called God, and a lady answered the phone. I said, 'This is Richard Haynes, I'm down in Amarillo, and I just got a letter from God. Is he in?' She said, 'What makes you think God is a *HE*?' I said, 'I'm just male chauvinist pig enough to think that.' The lady got on the phone and I told her, 'I got your letter and I appreciate your help, but I'm kind of like a lot of people in the Good Book, my memory is jaded, I need a sign.' She said, 'What kind of sign?' I said, 'Give me a numbered bank account in a Swiss bank.' She said, 'No.' I said, 'Lady, do this. When I read the Good Book, I find that boils were prevalent. If you can put a boil on the nose of Joe Cannon, my antagonist in this trial, I'd appreciate it. I don't want surgery. I don't want to disfigure him. I just want a boil on his nose.' She said, 'OKAY.' The next day when I see Joe, I said, 'Joe, you're giggling now, smart ass, but you're going to have a boil on your nose before the week is over.'"

I asked Racehorse if he ever got the boil and he shook his head. "He didn't, but his co-counsel, Marvin Collins, who later became a judge, had a boil on his butt. I said that was a pretty close shot for Odessa, Texas. I know Marvin has always got his nose up Joe's butt."

Racehorse never lost his sense of humor, but the case that really was the most important to him of all, after all the big cases, the mega-publicity, and notoriety he had gained in his life, it came down to a simple case that illustrates his LEAD line: He says, "It was a case I tried years ago. Mr. Jackson, a black man, was accused of stealing property from the jobsite where he worked. He worked with a bunch of white men, and I'm satisfied that the white guys were doing the stealing and blaming it on the black guy because he was the only black guy there. The jury acquitted him. The family had a little party for me at their house. They lived in the Third Ward in a one-bedroom shack. They had some people over there and they put my name on the wall. The kids had written, "God Bless Lawer Racehorse." They couldn't spell lawyer. They thanked me that night and I left there feeling that I have done something good. I've changed this man's life. It may have been the biggest victory I ever had. It made me feel good."

Racehorse's story confirmed my belief that the little things like making a difference in someone's life is what drives us as lawyers. It is not always the big stuff—the money and the fame—that gets us, it's knowing that we can help people and that things are different for that person because of the work we do. Racehorse will be remembered for having taken the mantle of Percy Foreman, the famous trial lawyer, and carrying it further than anyone ever thought he could. His creativity and reliance on people's good common sense made him a lawyer to be feared in the courtroom and revered by those he represented. He is an inspiration to us all.

# Freedom Requires Perseverance

*Walter H. White, Jr.*

Walter is from a family with a distinguished educational history. His father was an African American and Native American who went to Howard University Dental School in Washington, DC. Walter's mother's family was highly educated too. His maternal grandmother and her mother both had graduate level studies. His grandfather, Frederick Parker, attended Amherst College where he graduated in 1920 with the distinction *magna cum laude* in math and minors in chemistry and Latin. He went on to do graduate work at Harvard University and then he did additional graduate work at the Indiana University and he taught in the Indianapolis Public School system, where he headed up the math department for the segregated schools. He was dedicated to the desegregation of school systems.

When his mother went to college at Purdue University with his aunt Frieda, they had to take the fight to live in the dormitories to the governor. The university rules were that all freshman women were required to live in the dormitories. Winifred and Frieda were the first African American women to do so. They were brilliant people. He says, "I was raised in an environment where I was told that despite what the outside world thought, I was talented enough to do what I wanted to do and that no one could tell us otherwise."

Walter was fortunate to get that from both sides of his family. His mother was a microbiologist and when he was very young, she worked for the county medical center and she was a leader in the NAACP, the League of Women

Voters, the Urban League, and generally supported civil rights initiatives. He says, "I met Martin Luther King when I was quite young in the 1950s. I heard him speak and I got to sit on his lap when we met with him behind the stage. I met Thurgood Marshall and other distinguished lawyers, and my grandparents and my parents made sure that I was aware of both leaders and all of the major events in the civil rights movement."

As a child, Walter watched the marches in the South with great interest. His family actively supported the NAACP Legal Defense Fund. They marched when there were events in Milwaukee to desegregate housing in the southern part of the city. They campaigned for open housing laws. He says, "If there was a religion in my family, my parents were Christians, but an even stronger religion was education and black people's obligation to obtain a good education. Much of our lives evolved around our education. I knew when I was three years old that I was going to go to college."

Walter had a severe stuttering problem when he was young. He had a lot to say but nobody could understand him. He did speech therapy in school and on the weekends, he went to what was then called a school for the disabled, where most of the people were far more disabled than he was. There were people who didn't have limbs, who had serious mental challenges from autism to Down syndrome, blind people, and deaf people. After several years, he stopped going to the school for the disabled and his parents put him and his sister in drama classes. His sister was a serious young actress and is still involved in the television and film industry today. Walter was sent to learn to speak. He took a speech class and gave a speech on the radical Black Panthers and why it was important to listen to them. His speech teacher said, "You are signing up for the debate team." That's how he got into debate. When speaking about a subject he is passionate about, his childhood stutter went away.

When he was in junior high, they moved to a northern suburb of Milwaukee called Mequon where there were few African Americans. It was very different than the integrated community in Milwaukee where he had been. Some of the neighbors, but not all, did not take kindly to their presence. The first thing that he noticed was that his parents refused to let him answer the telephone. His father acquired a gun for protection in the event his disgruntled neighbors got seriously out of line. In the long run, the neighbors moved out. It was traumatic for him at the time. The problems at school were there but according to Walter they "were not transformational." He says, "For the most part, I was well received and made good friends. I ran for president of my class in the eighth grade and didn't win. Over time, the people of Mequon became my friends. We grew into the community in a very significant way. My parents were very active in community activities."

It was fortunate that he took Russian in high school because he would be able to use it later in life as a lawyer. He was aware of the cold war with Russia back then and was interested in what was happening on the other side and found the literature fascinating. He had a great admiration for and fascination with Alexander Pushkin.

He says, "The strength in light of the oppression and the brilliance under censorship appealed to me. I enjoyed the complexity. I enjoyed the moral stories, despite the horrors of the Soviet era. It was also fascinating to me at that time to realize that the greatest Russian poet was born of the African diaspora. Pushkin has the equivalent of Shakespeare in the Russian language. While Shakespeare is arguably the pinnacle of the English language, Pushkin was recognized for making the Russian language a literary language. He is the founder of the genre of the Great Russian literature, which, of course is, in my personal opinion, dynamic. And, he was of African descent. His grandmother was allegedly a gift from Hannibal to the Court of Peter the Great. She was an African anomaly, but she was openly accepted into the court and Pushkin was her progeny. In Russia, Pushkin was considered African. In fact, while Pushkin grew up in the court, he was recognized as being of African descent."

Although Walter definitely felt the impact of racial discrimination, he says, "Quite honestly, the impact on us, while significant, was nothing like the impact that it must have had on my parents and my grandparents. My grandfather used to tell the story of trying to vote in the South. He would go up to the poll and give his identification and they would say, 'You need more identification.' He would give them more identification and they would say, 'You have to take a test.' He would say, 'Okay.' Then they would ask, 'Can you read this in French?' and he would read it in French and translate it. His minor in Latin came in very handy. Then they would say, 'Can you read this in Spanish?' and he would read it in Spanish and translate it. They would say, 'Can you read this in Latin?' and he would read it and laugh, then translate it. This was the guy who used to write papers in Latin. Then they handed him the card in Chinese and say, 'Can you read this?' and he would finally say, 'I guess it says, I don't get to vote.'"

Listening to that story really had an impact on Walter. He says, "When you think of an individual who had all the pride and intelligence that he had, suffering these indignities, it caused me great pain. What my parents and grandparents made sure of is that we understood the pain and that we never accepted those indignities for ourselves. We would challenge people. I have indelible images of my grandfather, if he was taking the train in Georgia, he would go to the white booth to buy a ticket, and only after demanding a full ticket would he go back to the black booth and buy a ticket."

His grandfather was an educator at Yale. He ultimately received an award from Harvard College called the Distinguished Secondary Teaching Award, and he was awarded an honorary doctorate from Amherst College for the work that he had done. Walter remembers, "As I grew up, we had extraordinary access to academic institutions because my grandfather was a professor. After he retired from Yale, when I was in junior high school, he taught in Cedar Rapids at Coe College. We had the luxury of a very healthy family environment."

In high school, he studied in Finland through the American Field Service Program. It was as close as they could get him to Russia. At the time, there wasn't anything published about Russia except Communist propaganda. He brought back pictures of Stalin, which became very controversial. He says, "It was a very traumatic time for the United States because it was the middle of the Vietnam War during the Nixon administration. The views of Europe from the US were not positive ones. Finland was a fascinating learning experience. I realized that there is another world out there."

Then in college he traveled to Russia in 1973 with a group of college students. Political science was his fascination and anything Russian was his hobby, his passion. He completed a degree in Russian. As far as going to law school, there were no lawyers in his family. His family was educators, scientists, and businesspeople. He is the first lawyer in the family.

He did not find many courses in law school that he was passionate about. He says, "Law school has a way of distilling the passion from the exercise." He found issues relating to public international law fascinating—issues like how you achieve resolutions between border conflicts between states; international conventions; and treaties. Law school was challenging, but it wasn't as exciting as he thought it was going to be, because he was grappling with artificial issues as opposed to real issues.

Walter understood why he wanted to be a lawyer and he had a particular view of the concepts of justice, but a lot of it had to do with not accepting the law as written. He believed in the Rule of Law when it was just. Given his family, he was not brought up to think that either the law or the state was correct. He says, "The law was to be respected, but it was not to be recognized as infallible. The people who administered the law were people; they were not the law itself. The concept of the rule of laws as opposed to the rule of men was very, very strong in my family."

He became very active in the American Bar Association Young Lawyers Division and became chair in 1989–90. He has also been chair of the Milwaukee Young Lawyers Association, chair of the ABA Civil Rights and Social Justice Section and chair of the ABA Center for Human Rights. In 1988 he became commissioner of securities for the State of Wisconsin. Around that time changes were taking place in the former Soviet Union and he got involved in what was going on in Russia and saw there was a need for greater cooperation between the international regulators. He worked closely with the SEC and with the Canadian provincial regulators. He also worked with the British, French, and Japanese regulators. He also relished the opportunity to speak about regulatory activity in the securities market and the development of regulations in the Soviet Union, and ultimately the Russian Federation as well as newly independent states.

When he left the commissioner of securities office, he looked at firms who were doing business in Russia, and he decided that the market wasn't ready. He says, "Nobody was making money. It was still a very high-risk proposition. I joined Quarles & Brady, a Wisconsin firm that was very well regarded in securities work. They were large enough to engage in serious international activity." He did some work in South Africa but found himself back in Wisconsin when he got a call from a firm who needed someone to run their international operations, which included a large office in Moscow.

In 1994, he took his family first to Washington and then to Moscow and he became the head of Steptoe & Johnson International. He loved it because it was what he was trained to do. He was fascinated by Russia, he had lots of friends there, and Russia was going through an exciting change, it was a dynamic and a hopeful place. "But," he says, "it was very difficult on my family."

Walter was in the heyday of his career. He had a world-class group of lawyers in several countries and they were doing work that had never been done before. It was complex, multilingual, and multinational. They handled multi-billion-dollar investments into natural resource companies, multi-billion-dollar pipeline consortia, and they represented leading investment banks, funds, and leading global clients. What more could a lawyer trained and prepared for this moment want?

But the experience did not come without challenges. The first weekend that they moved into their apartment, a bomb went off in their building. They witnessed gun fights in the streets between criminal groups and the militia. His family required security support. He and his son had to take cover when shots were fired at his golf club.

But the most serious incident happened one day the night before the Super Bowl. His son went sledding on Sparrow Hills just below Moscow State University. He hit a pole and fractured his skull. He went to the American Medical Clinic where they said that they could not help him and that he was too far gone. Walter called his brother-in-law, who was on the medical faculty of Northwestern Medical School. Dr. Faines said to get him to a pediatric neurosurgeon immediately. Walter found one and they operated. A few days later Sasha was flown on a flying intensive care unit to Great Ormond Street Hospital in London, one of the leading pediatric medical facilities in the world. His son, Sasha, is fine and now and is an assistant professor at Johns Hopkins.

Walter knew that he could no longer expect his family to live in Moscow. He moved his family to London in 1997 and by 1999 he also moved to London and left Steptoe & Johnson as it really needed to be run from Moscow. My respect for Walter is immense because he chose his family over his lifelong dedication to Russia and he gave up his dream job to be close to his family, which is the best decision. It is what a good leader will do.

Walter has been a partner in several world-class firms. He has had fascinating clients, from global corporate players to emerging and frontier markets investors; to extraordinary entrepreneurs to Romani beneficiaries of reparations arising from activities in Nazi Germany. In his humility he doesn't think he has done enough to make a dent in the injustice in the world. He says, "As I look at the efforts of my great grandparents, my grandparents, my parents, and my son and daughter-in-law, I am forced to recognize that justice is a long game. It requires perseverance and a lifetime commitment. The forces of injustice are relentless. One must never yield to their demands."

# Never, Ever Give Up

*Melanie Bragg*

My story began in Dallas, Texas, in 1965 when I wrote the "Story of My Life" on my mother's manual typewriter and used the red ink. It was only a half a page, but the seeds were set for me to become a writer. I knew I wanted to tell my story. My mother, Lee Mayfield, got me a little French desk and I remember being so happy in my room working on all of my projects! Back then, I had the original smartphone in the form of a book, a little spiral notebook, and a pencil with me at all times. Somehow, even at an early age, I had the distinct sense that writing was my destiny.

From the beginning, reading was my passion. My paternal grandmother, Francis "Honey" Bragg, read to me nonstop. During our trips to West Texas to see our grandparents in the summer we would get bundled up in the big feather bed and she would read me the Brer Rabbit stories. I remember the joy I felt when I was able to take over and read to her. It was an idyllic late 1950s, early 1960s childhood—until the middle of third grade.

My first and most formative defining moment was the winter day in Dallas in 1965 where we had snow. Dad took my two younger brothers and me to build a snowman. When we returned, we were excited to tell Mom about it and when we burst through the door, I saw Honey standing by the fireplace with the saddest look on her face. I then glanced at the kitchen where my late Aunt Jean stood loading the dishwasher, also with a sad look on her face. I knew then that something bad happened. "Where's Mom?" Silence. Someone said, "Your Mom's not coming home." I can still feel the hollow pain those words instilled in me.

That was the day that my childhood was over. My innocence was lost. And everything that has happened since then in my life stems from that moment. I soon learned that I was strong and capable and very good at taking care of others. I learned that I could take care of myself. And even at that young age I saw that my father, Charles Bragg, had all of the cards—the job, the parents who were willing to come help take care of us, and the strength to handle three young children. My mother was ill, beaten down, her parents were already dead, and she had no marketable skills. As a little girl listening to the swirls of adult conversations around me, I made a vow that I was never going to be in the position that my mother found herself in with my father. I was grateful that I had a father who could take care of us, but it was still a completely new reality for us all.

My career was born that day and my fierce independence has been something I cherish. Like my peer group, I put myself through college and law school. Before I landed a prestigious law clerk job at Pennzoil Company, I waited tables and as I served "more chips," "more hot sauce," "more tea," I looked at the people in the restaurant eating their dinners and enjoying their holidays and said to myself, *I have a dream. I am going to be a lawyer and I am going to be one of these people sitting here and being served.* That dream kept me going through everything that followed.

A defining moment happened again on September 28, 1983, when I was involved in a bad car accident—I was not driving. In September, I had just finished my year as a briefing attorney for the 14th Court of Appeals and I had just opened my own practice. I had more cases than you could shake a stick at, and I was very enthusiastic and eager to serve the public and my profession. The accident happened in Cozumel, Mexico, and we were thrown from the vehicle. I landed on concrete. My body was covered in blood and dirt and I must have rolled some distance.

My injuries were severe, including a fractured skull from the top of my head to the base of my neck and a fractured sacrum bone. When I finally got home to the States, I was in the hospital for two weeks. My doctor said I was a miracle and proceeded to give me the worst medical prognosis that I have ever heard. I disagreed with him from the beginning and completely dismissed it as I ran out the door. He said that I had a great chance of dying an early death, having a stroke, and would have migraine headaches the rest of my life. I remember looking at him and shaking my head and thinking, *Oh no. That is not my story. I didn't work my way through college and law school for this to be my story.*

Fortune was looking my way because a judge I knew had a son who had a head injury and he knew better than I did what I was going through. He began to give me cases where all I had to do was go out to the house and make sure someone was okay and then report back to the court. I began to do the kind of work where I didn't have to read much because I could not retain information very well at first. I had been an avid reader with the goal of being an author and now I could barely comprehend a paragraph. Never mind the next accident four months later and the ensuing insult-to-injuries that occurred. All with the same driver of accident number one.

To cope, I dug myself into work. At that time, I was doing court-appointed work on behalf of elderly folks and children, which became my specialty along with morning criminal appointments. I showed up every day and success happened. A few years later I became the first woman president of Houston Young Lawyers Association and was active in bar work on the state and national levels.

By then I had achieved so much, but one day I said to myself, *My body isn't right.* I went into intense physical therapy and got my occipital bone popped back out so my spinal cord fluid could move normally. It was the biggest relief. And soon thereafter, I was able to read and write like I had before the accident. The whole thing is one of those unexplained medical miracles. I was very, very lucky. I still have problems with my neck and back, but I chalk them up to being "the price I pay for being alive." Life experiences like those are never far from your mind but they make you appreciate your life.

The defining moment of my mission in life as a lawyer came early in my legal career. Back in 1987 I worked with the probate courts and got appointed as temporary guardian or guardian of indigent wards of the state who were referred by Adult Protective Services. One cold, rainy Friday afternoon in December I was about to take off for several Christmas parties and I got a call from the court saying I had been appointed temporary guardian of a man named Leroy Foreman. I had to shift gears and run down to the court to pick up my order appointing me as temporary guardian. When I got to the court the judge said that I immediately needed to find out if the man was in the home because the electricity had been cut off and the man's "nephew"—not sure if it was a blood or kinship relationship—was on drugs and could be there with a gun.

*Oh great!* I thought. *Sounds like a lovely assignment.*

Now this was in the late 1980s and so you can imagine me with the big Texas hair and the sassy outfit in my cute little sports car heading out to the other side of the tracks. Literally, this place was in a cul-de-sac and there was a railroad track right there. This was the worst neighborhood in town and the most remote location I could imagine. Since I had a mobile phone back then (yes, it was a big chunky one built into my car), I called 911 and asked for a fire truck and an ambulance. I knew I might need backup and frankly I was a little scared. I had never done anything like this before.

When I arrived, the fire truck, ambulance, and a couple of police cars were there. The rain was cold, and it began to pour. The cops told me to sit in the car and they would see if anyone was in the house. A few minutes later they came and knocked on my window and said, "Ma'am, there is no one home. We knocked on the door so there is nothing else we can do."

In that moment, something rose up in me and I pulled out my order and said in the strongest voice I didn't know I had, "This order from the court makes me the guardian of Mr. Leroy Foreman and the court ordered me to find him and make sure he is alive and well. We need to bust the door down so please get it done now. I hope he's alive."

There was a strength and conviction in my voice that surprised even me, and the cops looked at one another and then marched back over to the house and broke in the back door of the dark house. A few minutes later they called out to me, "Ms. Bragg, come over here, you need to see something. We found him." They covered me from the rain and as I entered the dark, cold home they held a big flashlight over my head so I could make my way through the house.

Cowering on the couch, I saw a little old man in soiled clothes frantically crying out, "He took my money, he took all my money, my nephew . . . " The policemen put him on a stretcher and as they were carrying him out, I realized he was blind and very much in distress. When he passed by me, I placed my warm hand firmly on his heart and leaned into him and began to talk to him in a soft, gentle voice that I hoped he could trust. "Mr. Foreman, my name is Melanie Bragg. I am your guardian. You are on your way to the doctor and I am coming with you. I am going to take care of you."

When I placed my hand on his heart, said those words and felt him calming down, I felt a surge of power transfer between us and the words *white angel* echoed in my head. I knew in that moment that everything I had been through in my life had prepared me to be the lawyer I am and that the law was my calling, not just a job or a profession, but something that is deeply meaningful to the people I serve and to me personally.

The work I do today is still much the same and I still take those responsibilities very seriously. Helping those segments of our culture who don't have a voice—the elderly, the children, and the mentally disadvantaged is supremely fulfilling to me. And although I am not a mega-millionaire—yet—I am for sure a millionaire in the spirit. That is what matters to me—knowing I am living my life's purpose. And throughout my thirty-six years as a lawyer, I know that the key to success in life is to *Never, Ever Give Up.*

# Conclusion

Like everyone else, lawyers come in all shapes and sizes and from a variety of different backgrounds. Sometimes a stable home life produces great leaders. Sometimes a tough background produces great leaders. The commonalities among great leaders are that they overcome adversity, they keep going no matter what, they look at the circumstances and find alternatives, and they keep moving on. They take action.

The one driving force in all of the stories is the awareness of and dedication to public service. It is a supreme joy for most people to be dedicated to something outside themselves and to work toward a goal that is bigger than they could fathom alone. It is what binds us together as a profession, as a culture, as a world.

I am privileged and honored to bring you these stories of people that I consider some of the legal giants in America today. There are many more. Each story is unique and valuable. What I realized is that we all have commonalities that we become aware of as we listen to each other's stories. I was amazed during the interviews at how many experiences we had that were similar. I had a pattern of raising my hand in my office when the interviewee said something I related to or that I had experienced. If you could have been a fly on the wall you would have seen my hand going up over and over during the interviews. I had no idea that so many of my close friends had been through the same things I had—maybe not the facts, but the feelings and emotions around the experiences were the same.

I am excited about teaching the principles of these LEAD lines and spreading the word about how to be the best lawyer and leader you can be. Listening to others and really hearing their stories is a valuable skill. I urge you to think about the defining moments of your life and how they have shaped you. Have you turned them into the life of meaning and fulfillment you always dreamed of? I hope so. But if not, the work has just begun. Write down your thoughts. Talk about them to friends.

Appreciate yourself for all the good you have done. And then, give a hand to your fellow man. A smile. A light touch. A hug. All forms of positive communication can change the world. It is a worthwhile journey and the law is the path to follow.

# Biographies

*Dear Reader,*

*I wanted you to know a little bit about the interviewees in this book, but as you might guess, putting in a full bio of each one of them would span many pages and possibly be longer than the book itself. We have shortened them to a few highlights and will leave it to you to explore further the ones you are most interested in. There are many sources of information for some of them. I have included my personal connection to each of them, so you would know why they were chosen for this book.*

*—Melanie Bragg*

## Benes Z. Aldana

President and Chief Executive Officer at The National Judicial College, Reno, NV. Former Chief Trial Judge of the US Coast Guard. Benes was Chair of the Solo, Small Firm & General Practice Division of the ABA in from 2012 to 2013. He held his planning meeting in London at the Law Society, and we were able to travel together for the 800-year anniversary of the Magna Carta. Benes is a tireless public servant and a man dedicated to public service and civility.

*—www.linkedin.com/in/benes-aldana-13ba7b5/*

## Jeffrey M. Allen

Principal in the general practice law firm of Graves & Allen in Oakland, CA. Jeff is Editor of *GPSolo Magazine* and oversees the GPSolo eReport. Since he took over, the magazine has won numerous awards. He is the author of several books, mostly on technology, and writes with his coauthor, Ashley Hallene. They do a very popular program—60 Tips in 60 Minutes.

*—www.gravesallen.com/attorney-profile/*

## Dennis W. Archer

Chairman Emeritus at Dickinson Wright LLP in Detroit, MI. Former President of the American Bar Association (2003–2004), former Mayor of Detroit (1994–2001), and former Associate Justice, Michigan Supreme Court (1986–1990).

Dennis was Chair of the Solo, Small Firm & General Practice Division from 1987 to 1988 and one of the first ABA President-Elect's that I interviewed many years ago for my ABA YLD Fellows publication, *Fellows Fodder*. He is a hard worker and teacher at heart, and it is an honor to know him. He is one of the gentlest and kindest people I know. It is a privilege to include him in the book.

*—www.dickinson-wright.com/our-people/dennisw_archer?tab=0*

## Robert Armstrong

President and Cofounder of the American Academy of Estate Planning Attorneys (AAEPA), San Diego, CA. The book *The EMyth Attorney: Why Most Legal Practices Don't Work and What You Can Do About It* by Michael E. Gerber, Robert Armstrong, and Sanford M. Fisch has helped many attorneys—it is how I discovered Robert's great work and why I sought to interview him. I loved his story and his willingness to be so transparent.

*—www.aaepa.com/our-team/robert-armstrong/*

## Laurel G. Bellows

Founder and Managing Principal of The Bellows Law Group, P.C. in Chicago, IL. Former President of the American Bar Association (2012–2013). I have admired Laurel's kindness and energy and zest for life for a long time. The amazing things she has done in her life and the odds she has overcome are an inspiration to us all, especially in the area of women lawyers.

*—www.bellowslaw.com/laurel-g-bellows/*

## Talmage Boston

Partner at Shackelford, Bowen, McKinley & Norton, LLP, in Dallas, TX. Author of *Raising the Bar: The Crucial Role of the Lawyer in Society*. I met Talmage when he was leading author programs at the ABA Annual Meeting. He has published with the State Bar of Texas and is a fine lawyer and an inspiration to all.

*—https://shackelford.law/profiles/talmage-boston/*

## Melanie Bragg

Principal in the general civil law firm of Bragg Law PC, Houston, TX. Bragg is Chair of the ABA Solo, Small Firm & General Practice Division and former Chair of the Book Publications Board. Bragg serves on the Board of Directors of the Texas Bar Foundation and is the author of *HIPAA for the General*

*Practitioner* and *Crosstown Park*, an Alex Stockton legal thriller. She is a frequent speaker and workshop leader.

*—www.bragglawpc.com/attorney/melanie-bragg/*

## Hon. Pamila J. Brown
Administrative Judge for the District Court of Maryland, District Ten, Ellicott City, MD. Judge Brown is a long-time public servant and active ABA member. Over the years, she has devoted a lot of her time and energy to domestic violence, as well as many other subjects. We have been friends since the Young Lawyers Division days and she is a gem of a person, through and through.

## Tabitha M. Charlton
Chief Operating Officer at Boudreaux Hunter & Associates, LLC, Houston, TX. Tabitha's story really interested me because I have done Children's Protective Services work for many years and am very aware of the problem with foster children finding good homes. Her charity, Kidsave, is something I support and hope that it will be a model for other communities. She is an example of what good can come from a tough past.

*—https://bhlawtexas.com/our-attorneys/tabitha-charlton/*

## John W. Clark, Jr.
Practitioner in business transactional law and oil and gas law, and advisor in legal matters stemming from the consequences of alcohol and drug abuse at The Clark Law Firm, Dallas, TX. John is a former Chair of the ABA Solo, Small Firm & General Practice Division (1995–1996) and has been a subject of my interviews for the YLD publication, *Fellows Fodder*. His candor and honesty about his past and how he uses the lessons he learned the hard way are why his interview is so special to me. He welcomes anyone who sees themselves in his interview.

*—www.clarklawfirm.net/staff.html*

## Sandy D'Alemberte
President Emeritus, Florida State University; Professor and former Dean, Florida State University College of Law, Tallahassee, FL. Former President of the American Bar Association (1991–1992). Sandy is a good friend of my friend, Bill Ide. I was very honored when he said yes to the interview and talked about his life so candidly.

*—https://law.fsu.edu/faculty-staff/talbot-sandy-dalemberte*

## Laura V. Farber

Partner and member of the Litigation and Employment Practice Groups at Hahn & Hahn LLP in Pasadena, CA. Laura was Chair of the Young Lawyers Division of the ABA. I was always impressed by her ability to handle many different tasks at once, namely being a young mother of two while running a national organization. She was Chair of the Solo, Small Firm & General Practice Division from 2011 to 2012. I am very proud of all she does to make the world a better place, including being President and Chairman of the Board for 2019 to 2020 Pasadena Tournament of the Roses.

*—www.hahnlawyers.com/laura-v-farber*

## Michael S. Greco

Retired Partner in the Boston office of K&L Gates LLP, serving as a trial lawyer, arbitrator, and mediator. Former President of the American Bar Association (2005–2006). Michael is a lawyer who didn't come up in the ABA through the Young Lawyers Division and it was a highlight for William Hubbard, former YLD Chair and former ABA President, and I to confer upon him the honorary Young Lawyer Division membership at the YLD Assembly when he was President of the ABA. His interview was so moving, and he feels so deeply about the subjects he invests his life in, namely human rights.

*—www.klgates.com/michael-s-greco/*

## Robert J. Grey, Jr.

Senior Counsel, Retired, at Hunton Andrews Kurth in Richmond, VA, and Washington, DC. Former President of the American Bar Association (2004–2005). Robert Grey grew up down the street from Thurgood Marshall and has spent his life serving his community and his profession. I first met him when I interviewed him for the YLD *Fellows Fodder* when he was President-Elect of the ABA. He is a man of many talents and exceptional contributions to the profession.

*—www.huntonak.com/en/people/robert-grey.html*

## Christopher L. Griffin

Retired Partner and business litigation lawyer with Foley & Lardner LLP in the firm's Tampa Bay, FL, office. Chris was YLD Chair from 1988 to 1989. He has been an outstanding advocate in the ABA for women's rights and an outstanding lawyer. He now enjoys time with his grandkids and mediates cases.

*—www.foley.com/christopher-l-griffin/*

## Richard "Racehorse" Haynes

Late criminal defense attorney at Richard Haynes & Associates in Houston, TX, and widely known for a series of difficult murder trials in Texas in the 1970s and 1980s. Racehorse had a well-earned reputation in Houston and around the world for being one of the best trial lawyers ever. He was famous for his cross-examination. His story-telling skills were second to none. He was in his 80s at the time of my interview. He always had a twinkle in his eye and a joke to tell. He never acted like the legendary lawyer he truly was. He is so missed by all who knew him.

*—https://en.wikipedia.org/wiki/Richard_Haynes_(lawyer)*

## Cindy K. Hide

Principal in the boutique Family Law firm of Cindy K. Hide, LLC in Houston, TX. Cindy is a woman who has taken her many life experiences and turned them into her company *Love, Money & the Law*. She strives to help women create their best lives with her workshops, appearances, and publications.

*—www.cindyhidelaw.com/*

## Kathleen Hopkins

Commercial Real Estate Attorney at Real Property Law Group, PLLC in Seattle, WA. Anyone who knows Kathleen knows she is a whirlwind of productivity. She is always tackling every problem she can solve, every event she can create, and all in the effort to serve her family, her friends, and her profession. We have worked together in the ABA for many years. She is so smart I have to ask her to slow down so I can compute what she is saying. Kathleen has a zest for life like no other and does not let anything get her down.

*—http://rp-lawgroup.com/team_members/kathleen-hopkins/*

## Pamela Fagan Hutchins

Texas attorney and author of award-winning and bestselling romantic mysteries, as well as nonfiction. Pamela is a woman's woman and I love the fact that she told the truth about the curse of beauty as a girl and later as a woman. It is a story few dare to tell, but Pamela has gained her incredible following by telling the truth about everything in her life. She is the most transparent person I know, and one of the smartest. I learned in her interview about her speed writing as a youngster and sure wish I had known about that. She and her husband, Eric, bought an RV and travelled the country to promote her novels. She is an award-winning novelist and teaches at writing conferences.

*—https://pamelafaganhutchins.com/about-2/*

## R. William "Bill" Ide, III

Partner in the Atlanta, GA, office of Dentons. Former President of the American Bar Association (1994–1995). Bill became my friend when I interviewed him for the YLD *Fellows Fodder*. He has such a great background and story and is a man of many talents. His overall love of community service and corporate responsibility as well as his commitment to personal growth are why I wanted him to be a part of this project.

*—www.dentons.com/en/bill-ide*

## Nina L. Kaufman

New York City business attorney, author, and former stand-up comic. Nina is someone I know through our mutual self-growth and empowerment work. I saw her in some of my groups and got to know her via email and online and was impressed with her body of work in the area of helping lawyers succeed. She knows how to lead by example.

*—www.linkedin.com/in/ninakaufman/*

## Hon. John Kralik

Judge of the Superior Court of Los Angeles County, CA, and best-selling author of *A Simple Act of Gratitude: How Learning to Say Thank You Changed My Life*. I read Judge Kralik's book, *365 Thank You's*, and was very impressed by a lawyer who finally told the truth about the lives we live and the stress that is upon us each and every day. The fact that such a simple act as writing a thank you note a day changed his life is an amazing story. I had the good fortune of meeting him, going to his courtroom and seeing him in action. It is an honor to have him in the book.

## Alan Kopit

Executive Vice President and General Counsel at MediLogix, LLC, and former Partner in Charge at Hahn Loeser & Parks LLP in Cleveland, OH. Alan and I have been friends for many years from our ABA Young Lawyers Division days. He is known for his television broadcast work and is one of the nicest and most successful men you will ever meet.

*—www.linkedin.com/in/alan-kopit-91b84715/*

## Scott C. LaBarre

Owner and Operator of LaBarre Law Offices P.C. in Denver, CO. Scott is a friend from the ABA Young Lawyers Division and the Solo, Small Firm & General Practice Division. He is one of the smartest men and most eloquent speakers I have ever met. I love how he doesn't want to be treated any differently because he is blind. He is funny and accomplished and a joy to be around. He will make a great Chair of the ABA Solo, Small Firm & General Practice Division.

*—www.labarrelaw.com/about.html*

## Mark Lane

Late defense lawyer, social activist, and author known for his 1966 critique of the Warren Commission, *Rush to Judgment*. Mark Lane was around 84 when I talked to him, and his autobiography, *Citizen Lane*, had just come out. I was fascinated by the fact that he was Jim Jones' lawyer and that he went down to Guyana and was there during the mass suicide and he survived. He was also in the freedom rides in the Civil Rights movement and was hanging out with a mutual friend, Carolyn Mugar. He had a very interesting and meaningful life.

*—https://en.wikipedia.org/wiki/Mark_Lane_(author)*

## Leslie H. Lowe

Late former Director of the Energy and Environment Program, the Interfaith Center on Corporate Responsibility, and a New York attorney specializing in environmental law and corporate environmental disclosure. She lived a great and exciting life that was cut short too soon. When I met her in 1976 in Paris, neither one of us knew we would be lawyers someday. We kept in touch through the years and shared an exciting past and laughed at our memories when we got together. She had won the Dick Clark $25,000 Pyramid Show when she was 24 so she went to Paris to study African History at the Sorbonne. It was her second master's degree. Leslie worked tirelessly to right many wrongs and she accomplished much in her life.

## John McKay

Chair of the Government Investigations and Crisis Management Group at Davis Wright Tremaine LLP and former US Attorney, Western District of Washington, in Seattle, WA. John was also a law school professor at the Seattle University School of Law and a White House Fellow. We served together in the ABA Young Lawyers Division and were honored to be directors for then Chair, Judy Perry Martinez. Being with John is always stimulating and fun, and he has the best attitude about life. I always learn something when I am with him.

*—www.dwt.com/people/johnmckay/*

## Judy Perry Martinez

Of Counsel at Simon, Peragine, Smith & Redfearn, LLP in New Orleans. President-Elect of the American Bar Association for 2019 to 2020. Judy is a woman whose passion and commitment to the practice of law, to lawyers, and to the public we serve is bar none; a cut above the norm. Her energy and brilliance in being able to work with a variety of groups of people to accomplish great things are unparalleled.

—*www.spsr-law.com/index.php/judy-perry-martinez*

## Karen J. Mathis

Former Partner with the law firm McElroy, Deutsch, Mulvaney & Carpenter, LLC. Former President of the American Bar Association (2006–2007). Karen was Chair of the Solo, Small Firm & General Practice Division from 2002 to 2003, the year before I got involved in what was then a Section. She is dynamic and full of energy with a heart for children as she served as CEO of Big Brothers Big Sisters of America for two and a half years.

—*https://en.wikipedia.org/wiki/Karen_J._Mathis*

## Barbara Mayden

Principal at the boutique legal recruiting firm Young Mayden, LLC in Nashville, TN. Practitioner for more than 30 years in Atlanta, New York, and Nashville. Barbara is a staunch supporter of women's rights and a former Chair of the ABA Business Law Section as well as Chair of the Young Lawyer's Division. She followed her dream of creating Young Mayden and now oversees prominent headhunting jobs all across America.

—*www.youngmayden.com/*

## Alan O. Olson

Principal at Olson Law Office, PC in Des Moines, IA. Alan is a former Chair of the Young Lawyers Division and one of the most successful and persuasive lawyers I know. He has a laugh as big as Dallas and serves as the Budget Director of the Solo, Small Firm & General Practice Division.

—*http://olson-law.net/profile/2020628*

## Jim Perdue, Sr.

Of Counsel to Perdue & Kidd in Houston, TX; dubbed by *Forbes* magazine as "King of the Malpractice Lawyers." Jim, or Mr. Perdue as I call him, is a legend in Texas and one of the most prominent medical malpractice lawyers who I have known since I got out of law school. His son, Jim, Jr. is a top lawyer and an active member of the state and local bar. Mr. Perdue teaches at University of Houston Law Center and shares his knowledge of storytelling in a special class created just for him and his students.

*—www.perdueandkidd.com/lawyers/jim-m-perdue-sr/*

## Wm. T. (Bill) Robinson, III

Late Member-in-Charge of the Northern Kentucky offices of Frost Brown Todd LLC. Former President of the American Bar Association (2011–2012). Bill was the kindest man you could ever meet, and it was such a pleasure to get to know him in the later stages of his life. He was so gracious in our interview and we found many things in common, such that we were friends until his death. His life and story about the power of intuition is one that I hope readers will love. Talking to him was always a wealth of knowledge.

*—www.frostbrowntodd.com/newsroom-press-former-*
*american-bar-association-president-and-local-*
*attorney-wm-t-bill-robinson-dies.html*

## Raquel "Rocky" A. Rodriguez

Managing Member at the Miami office of McDonald Hopkins LLC. Served as General Counsel to former Florida Governor Jeb Bush. Very few people impress me as much as Rocky. She was a powerhouse Chair of the Young Lawyers Division a few years after I "aged out," and we shared a love of anything international. I was with her when I discovered the Blackberry. She had this little black pager-looking thing in her hand and said, "They'll meet us in the bar." I asked how she knew, and she told me that little black thing sent email. It was a thrilling prospect to talk to people without having a phone call in real time. We have traveled together and eaten many fine meals together. Her zest for life and her pursuit of excellence make her unique and fun to be around, as well as being an awesome lawyer and leader.

*—https://mcdonaldhopkins.com/Team/*
*Attorney/r/Raquel-Rocky-Rodriguez*

## Scott E. Rozzell

Executive Vice President and General Counsel of CenterPoint Energy, Houston, TX, from 2001 until his retirement in 2014. Former Senior Partner and Chair of the Energy Department of the Houston office of Baker Botts LLP. Scott is someone I met back when I was in law school and we planned a host committee meeting for the Texas Young Lawyers Association. In fact, he appointed me to Chair my very first HYLA committee in 1986, the Law Day Committee, when he was President of Houston Young Lawyers Association. Always an adventurous soul, he is enjoying his retirement, his love of flying WWII planes, and trotting the globe learning new things about the cultures and peoples of the world.

*—http://investors.centerpointenergy.com/ executive-committee/scott-rozzell*

### Hon. Jennifer Rymell
Judge, County Court at Law Judge, Tarrant County, Fort Worth, TX. Judge Rymell was Chair of the Solo, Small Firm & General Practice Division from 2013 to 2014 and is a distinguished alumnus at St. Mary's University School of Law in San Antonio. Judge Jenny, as she is called, is smart, motivated, and eager to lend a hand on public service projects. We met through the Texas Young Lawyers Association and have been friends for many years. She has a laugh that is infectious. "Dedication" is a word that comes to mind when I think of her.

### Wilson Adam Schooley
Owner/Managing Partner of Schooley Law Firm, actor, author, magazine editor, and photographer in La Mesa, CA. Wil is a long-time friend going back to the ABA Young Lawyer Division days. Wil is currently the Chair of the ABA Civil Rights & Civil Justice Section and has a passion for diversity and gender bias education. He is a well-respected and admired friend to many. And he got to play Atticus Finch in *To Kill a Mockingbird*.

*—www.linkedin.com/in/wilson-adam-schooley-911b3517/*

### Hon. John V. Singleton, III
Late retired Chief Judge of the US District Court for the Southern District of Texas. Judge Singleton was one of the most interesting people I think I have ever met. He was funny and outrageous and just a hoot to work with. I was lucky, because for three years when I was a young lawyer, we worked on the Law Day luncheon and naturalization ceremony for new citizens together. He called his old friends, like former US Attorney General Griffin Bell and James Baker, to come speak. We even got Governor Mark White to come one year. He had a wealth of knowledge of politics and I learned so much from him over the years.

*—www.txs.uscourts.gov/page/judge-john-v-singleton-be-honored*

## Kent W. Spence

Third generation Wyomingite and principal of the Kent Spence Law Firm. I met Kent when his bar exam coach, my former law school professor, Peter Lewis, found out I was going to Jackson Hole for a bar association meeting. Kent's story of persistence was so compelling I never forgot. He has a passion for the law and helping the underdog and has earned his place in the legal profession.

*—www.kentspencelaw.com/about-us/*

## Dr. Artika R. Tyner

Associate Vice President, Office of Institutional Diversity, University of Saint Thomas, Minnesota. Dr. Tyner, or Artika to me, is a young woman with many accomplishments already under her belt. Never have I seen such a fervent passion to sow good in the world from a leader. She is an accomplished author of several leadership books and a children's book. She has a TEDTalk. It is a joy to be her friend and follow along with her in her journey to create good in the world.

*—www.linkedin.com/in/artikatyner/*

## Walter H. White, Jr.

International Advisor, London, United Kingdom. Former international business and finance lawyer at the London office of McGuireWoods. I met Walter back in my young lawyer days as he was Chair of the ABA Young Lawyers Division. The thing that always impressed me about Walter was how smart he was. He has an air about him that makes him very interesting to talk to. He has always been very involved in international work, especially Russia. I just couldn't leave the part of his interview out that covered Pushkin's heritage because I think that might be an interesting fact few people know. Walter never ceases to amaze me.

*—www.linkedin.com/in/walter-h-white-jr-70216aa/*

## Alan Yamamoto

Federal criminal defense lawyer at the Law Offices of Alan H. Yamamoto, Alexandria, VA. Alan is a man who has served in government and as a solo practitioner, but he got the case of a lifetime when the judge appointed him to represent one of the 9/11 terrorists. What he shared with me in our interview is so interesting to me in terms of the lesson about how our legal system works. I feel honored and lucky to have had the chance to include him in this book.

*—www.yamamotolaw.net/*